Workshop on Computational Semantics Beyond Events and Roles (SemBEaR 2018)

AA001511

New Orleans, Louisiana, USA
5 June 2018

ISBN: 978-1-5108-6362-0

Printed from e-media with permission by:

Curran Associates, Inc.
57 Morehouse Lane
Red Hook, NY 12571

CURRAN ASSOCIATES INC.
proceedings
.com

Some format issues inherent in the e-media version may also appear in this print version.

Copyright© (2018) by the Association for Computational Linguistics
All rights reserved.

Printed by Curran Associates, Inc. (2018)

For permission requests, please contact the Association for Computational Linguistics
at the address below.

Association for Computational Linguistics
209 N. Eighth Street
Stroudsburg, Pennsylvania 18360

Phone: 1-570-476-8006
Fax: 1-570-476-0860

acl@aclweb.org

Additional copies of this publication are available from:

Curran Associates, Inc.
57 Morehouse Lane
Red Hook, NY 12571 USA
Phone: 845-758-0400
Fax: 845-758-2633
Email: curran@proceedings.com
Web: www.proceedings.com

NAACL HLT 2018

Computational Semantics Beyond Events and Roles (SemBEaR 2018)

Proceedings of the Workshop

June 5, 2018
New Orleans, Louisiana

©2018 The Association for Computational Linguistics

Introduction

During the last decade, semantic representation of text has focused on extracting propositional meaning, i.e., capturing who does what to whom, how, when and where. Several corpora are available, and existing tools extract this kind of knowledge, e.g., role labelers trained on PropBank or NomBank. Nevertheless, most current representations tend to disregard significant meaning encoded in human language. For example, sentences 1-2 below share the same argument structure regarding verb contracted, but do not convey the same overall meaning. While in the first example John contracting the disease is factual, in the second it is not:

1. John likely contracted the disease when a mouse bit him in the Adirondacks.
2. John never contracted the disease although a mouse bit him in the Adirondacks.

In order to truly capture what these sentences mean, aspects of meaning that go beyond identifying events and their roles (e.g., uncertainty, negation and attribution) must be taken into account. The Workshop on Computational Semantics Beyond Events and Roles focuses on a broad range of semantic phenomena that lays beyond the identification and linking of eventualities and their semantic arguments with relations such as *agent* (who), *theme* (what) and *location* (where), here so called SemBEaR.

SemBEaR is pervasive in human language and, while studied from a theoretical perspective, computational models are still scarce. Humans use language to describe events that do not correlate with a real situation in the world. They express desires, intentions and plans, and also discuss events that did not happen or are unlikely to happen. Events are often described hypothetically, and speculation can be used to explain why something is a certain way without a strong commitment. Humans do not always (want to) tell the (whole) truth: they may use deception to hide lies. Devices such as irony and sarcasm are employed to play with words so that what is said is not what is meant. Finally, humans not only describe their personal views or experiences, but also attribute statements to others. These phenomena are not exclusive of opinionated texts, but they are ubiquitous in language, even in scientific works and news as exemplified in the sentences below:

- Female leaders might have avoided world wars.
- Political experts speculate that Donald Trump's meltdown is beginning.
- Infected people typically don't become contagious until they develop symptoms.
- Medical personnel can be infected if they don't use protective gear, such as surgical masks and gloves.
- You can only catch Ebola from coming into direct contact with the bodily fluids of someone who has the disease and is showing symptoms.
- We have never seen a human virus change the way it is transmitted.
- The government did not release the files until 1998.

In its 2018 edition, the Workshop on Computational Semantics Beyond Events and Roles (SemBEaR) brought together scientists working on these kind of semantic phenomena within computational semantics. The workshop was collocated with the 16th Annual Conference of the North American Chapter of the Association for Computational Linguistics: Human Language Technologies (NAACL 2018) in New Orleans, Louisiana, and took place on June 5, 2018. The program included papers SemBEaR 2018 is a follow-up of five previous events: the 2010 Negation and Speculation in Natural Language Processing Workshop (NeSp-NLP 2010), the Extra-Propositional Aspects of Meaning (ExProM) in Computational Linguistics Workshops held in 2012, 2015 and 2016, and SemBEaR 2017.

We would like to thank the authors of papers for their interesting contributions and the members of the program committee for their insightful reviews. We are also grateful to the National Science Foundation for a grant to support student travel to the workshop.

Eduardo Blanco, University of North Texas
Roser Morante, VU University Amsterdam
Workshop Co-Chairs

Organizers:

Eduardo Blanco - University of North Texas, USA
Roser Morante - VU University Amsterdam, The Netherlands

Program Committee:

Mithun Balakrishna - Lymba Corporation
Jorge Carrillo-de-Albornoz - Universidad Nacional de Eduación a Distancia
Tommaso Caselli - University of Groningen
Iris Hendrickx - Radboud University
Halil Kilicoglu - U.S. National Library of Medicine
Christopher Potts - Stanford University German Rigau - UPV/EHU
Josef Ruppenhofer - Heidelberg University
Erik Velldal - University of Oslo
Lilja Øvrelid - University of Oslo

Invited Speaker:

Ivan Habernal - UKP Lab, Technische Universität Darmstadt

Table of Contents

Workshop Program

Tuesday June 5, 2018

9:00–9:10 Opening Remarks

9:10–9:30 *Using Hedge Detection to Improve Committed Belief Tagging*
Morgan Ulinski, Seth Benjamin and Julia Hirschberg

9:30–10:00 *Paths for Uncertainty: Exploring the Intricacies of Uncertainty Identification for News*
Chrysoula Zerva and Sophia Ananiadou

10:00–10:20 *Detecting Sarcasm is Extremely Easy ;-)*
Natalie Parde and Rodney Nielsen

10:20–10:30 Discussion Session 1

10:30–11:00 Coffee Break

11:00–11:30 *GKR: the Graphical Knowledge Representation for semantic parsing*
Aikaterini-Lida Kalouli and Richard Crouch

Invited talk

11:30–12:20 *Computational Argumentation: A Journey Beyond Semantics, Logic, Opinions, and Easy Tasks*
Ivan Habernal

12:20–12:30 Discussion Session 2

Using Hedge Detection to Improve Committed Belief Tagging

Morgan Ulinski and **Seth Benjamin** and **Julia Hirschberg**
Department of Computer Science
Columbia University
New York, NY, USA
{mulinski@cs.,sjb2190@,julia@cs.}columbia.edu

Abstract

We describe a novel method for identifying hedge terms using a set of manually constructed rules. We present experiments adding hedge features to a committed belief system to improve classification. We compare performance of this system (a) without hedging features, (b) with dictionary-based features, and (c) with rule-based features. We find that using hedge features improves performance of the committed belief system, particularly in identifying instances of non-committed belief and reported belief.

1 Introduction

Hedging refers to the use of words, sounds, or constructions that add ambiguity or uncertainty to spoken or written language. Hedges are often used by speakers to indicate lack of commitment to what they say; so, the ability to classify words and phrases as hedges is very relevant to the task of committed belief tagging—that is, determining the level of commitment a speaker has toward the belief expressed in a given proposition. A major challenge in identifying hedges is that many hedge words and phrases are ambiguous. For example, In (1), *around* is used as a hedge, but not in (2).

(1) She weighs **around** a hundred pounds.

(2) Suddenly she turned **around**.

Currently there are few corpora annotated for hedging, and these are in a limited number of genres. In particular, there is currently no corpus of *informal* language annotated with hedge behavior. Acquiring expert annotations on text in other genres can be time consuming and may be cost prohibitive, which is an impediment to exploring how hedging can help with applications based on text and other genres. In this paper, the application we focus on is committed belief tagging on a corpus of forum posts. Since we currently lack a labeled hedging corpus in this genre, we introduce a new method for disambiguating potential hedges using a set of manually-constructed rules. We then show that detecting hedges using this method improves the performance of a committed belief tagger.

In Section 2, we discuss related work. In Section 3, we describe how we identify hedges. We describe the committed belief tagger used for our experiments in Section 4. In Section 5, we describe our experiments and our results. We conclude and discuss future work in Section 6.

2 Related Work

Most work on hedge detection has focused on using machine learning models based on annotated data, primarily from the domain of academic writing. The CoNLL-2010 shared task on learning to detect hedges (Farkas et al., 2010) used the BioScope corpus (Vincze et al., 2008) of biomedical abstracts and articles and a Wikipedia corpus annotated for "weasel words." Most CoNLL-2010 systems approach the task as a sequence labeling problem on the token level (e.g. Tang et al. (2010)); others approached it as a token-by-token classification problem (e.g. Vlachos and Craven (2010)) or as a sentence classification problem (e.g. Clausen (2010)).

Our approach is closest to Velldal (2011), a follow-up to CoNLL-2010 which frames the task of identifying hedges as a disambiguation problem in which all potential hedge cues are located and then subsequently disambiguated according to whether they are used as a hedge or not. However, our work differs in that we use a set of manually-constructed rules to disambiguate potential hedges rather than a machine learning classifier. Using a rule-based rather than machine-learning approach allows us to apply our hedge detection method to

Proceedings of the Workshop on Computational Semantics beyond Events and Roles (SemBEaR-2018), pages 1–5
New Orleans, Louisiana, June 5, 2018. ©2017 Association for Computational Linguistics

Relational Hedges	Propositional Hedges
according to, **appear**, arguably, **assume**, **believe**, **consider**, could, **doubt**, estimate, expect, **feel**, **find**, guess, hear, I mean, I would say, **imagine**, **impression**, in my mind, in my opinion, in my understanding, in my view, **know**, **likely**, look like, looks like, **may**, maybe, **might**, my thinking, my understanding, necessarily, perhaps, possibly, presumably, probably, read, say, seem, seemingly, **should**, sound like, sounds like, speculate, suggest, **suppose**, **sure**, **tend**, think, understand, **unlikely**, unsure	a bit, a bunch, a couple, a few, a little, a whole bunch, **about**, allegedly, among others, and all that, and so forth, and so on, and suchlike, apparently, approximately, around, at least, basic, basically, **completely**, et cetera, etc, **fair**, **fairly**, for the most part, frequently, **general**, generally, in a way, in part, in some ways, kind of, kinda, largely, **like**, mainly, more or less, **most**, mostly, much, occasionally, **often**, **partial**, partially, partly, **possible**, practically, **pretty**, pretty much, probable, rarely, **rather**, **really**, relatively, rough, **roughly**, seldom, several, something or other, sort of, to a certain extent, to some extent, **totally**, usually, virtually

Table 1: List of (potential) hedge words and phrases.

a corpus of forum posts that has not been annotated with hedge information. Our work also differs from previous efforts in that we are interested not just in the problem of hedge detection itself, but in its application to committed belief tagging.

3 Identifying Hedge Terms

We first compiled a dictionary of 117 potential hedge words and phrases. We began with the hedge terms identified during the CoNLL-2010 shared task (Farkas et al., 2010), along with synonyms of these terms extracted from WordNet. This list was further expanded and edited through consultation with the Linguistic Data Consortium (LDC) and other linguists. For each hedge term in our dictionary, we wrote definitions defining the hedging and non-hedging usages of the term. We use these definitions as the basis for the rules in our hedge classifier.

This hedging dictionary is divided into *relational* and *propositional* hedges. As described in Prokofieva and Hirschberg (2014), relational hedges have to do with the speaker's relation to the propositional content, while propositional hedges are those that introduce uncertainty into the propositional content itself. Consider the following:

(3) I **think** the ball is blue.

(4) The ball is **sort of** blue.

In (3), *think* is a relational hedge. In (4), *sort of* is a propositional hedge.

Our baseline hedge detector is a simple, *dictionary-based* one. Using our dictionary of potential hedge terms, we look up the lemma of each token in the dictionary and mark it as a hedge if found. This procedure, however, does not take into account the inherent ambiguity of many of the hedge terms. To handle this ambiguity, we implemented *rule-based* hedge detection. The rule-based system disambiguates hedge vs. non-hedge usages using rules based on context, part-of-speech, and dependency information.

The full list of hedge words and phrases in our dictionary is shown in Table 1. The hedge terms for which we have written rules are shown in bold; the rule-based system classifies others as hedges by default. Table 2 shows a sample of the rules, with examples of hedging and non-hedging uses.

We evaluate both dictionary-based and rule-based approaches in a committed belief tagger.

4 Committed Belief Tagger

We employ the committed belief tagger described in Prabhakaran et al. (2010) and as Sytem C in Prabhakaran et al. (2015). This tagger uses a quadratic kernel SVM to train a model using lexical and syntactic features. Tags are assigned at the word level; the tagger identifies tokens denoting the heads of propositions and classifies each proposition as one of four belief types:

- **Committed belief (CB):** the speaker-writer believes the proposition with certainty, e.g.

  (5) The sun will rise tomorrow.

  (6) I know John and Katie went to Paris last year.

- **Non-committed belief (NCB):** the speaker-writer believes the proposition to be possibly, but not necessarily, true, e.g.

Hedge term	Rule	Examples
about	If token t has part-of-speech IN, t is non-hedge. Otherwise, hedge.	Hedge: There are **about** 10 million packages in transit right now. Non-hedge: We need to talk **about** Mark.
likely	If token t has relation amod with its head h, and h has part-of-speech N*, t is non-hedge. Otherwise, hedge.	Hedge: We will **likely** stay home this evening. Non-hedge: He is a fine, **likely** young man.
rather	If token t is followed by token 'than', t is non-hedge. Otherwise, hedge.	Hedge: She's been behaving **rather** strangely. Non-hedge: She seemed indifferent **rather** than angry.
assume	If token t has ccomp dependent, t is hedge. Otherwise, non-hedge.	Hedge: I **assume** his train was late. Non-hedge: When will the president **assume** office?
tend	If token t has xcomp dependent, t is hedge. Otherwise, non-hedge.	Hedge: Written language **tends** to be formal. Non-hedge: Viola **tended** plants on the roof.
appear	If token t has xcomp or ccomp dependent, t is hedge. Otherwise, non-hedge.	Hedge: The problem **appears** to be a bug in the software. Non-hedge: A man suddenly **appeared** in the doorway.
sure	If token t has neg dependent, t is hedge. Otherwise, non-hedge.	Hedge: I'm not **sure** what the exact numbers are. Non-hedge: He is **sure** she will turn up tomorrow.
completely	If the head of token t has neg dependent, t is hedge. Otherwise, non-hedge.	Hedge: That isn't **completely** true. Non-hedge: I am **completely** sure you will win.
suppose	If token t has xcomp dependent d and d has mark dependent 'to', t is non-hedge. Otherwise, hedge.	Hedge: I **suppose** the package will arrive next week. Non-hedge: I'm **supposed** to call if I'm going to be late.
should	If token t has relation aux with its head h and h has dependent 'have', t is non-hedge. Otherwise, hedge.	Hedge: It **should** be rainy tomorrow. Non-hedge: He **should** have been more careful.

Table 2: Examples of rules used to disambiguate hedge terms.

(7) It could rain tomorrow.

(8) I think John and Katie went to Paris last year.

- **Reported belief (ROB):** the speaker-writer reports the belief as belonging to someone else, without specifying their own belief or lack of belief in the proposition, e.g.

(9) Channel 6 said it could rain tomorrow.

(10) Sarah said that John and Katie went to Paris last year.

- **Non-belief propositions (NA):** the speaker-writer expresses some cognitive attitude other than belief toward the proposition, such as desire, intention, or obligation, e.g.

(11) Is it going to rain tomorrow?

(12) I hope John and Katie went to Paris last year.

4.1 Hedge Features

For the experiments described in this paper, we add the following additional features to the committed belief tagger:

- **Word features**: based on properties of the current word being tagged. If the word is classified as a hedge by the hedge detector, , *HedgeLemma*, and *HedgeType* are set to the token, lemma, and hedge type (propositional or relational) of the word. Otherwise, these features are null.

- **Dependency features**: based on attributes of words related to the current word by the dependency parse. If the child of a given word is classified as a hedge by the hedge detector, *HedgeTokenChild*, *HedgeLemmaChild*, and *HedgeTypeChild* are set to the token, lemma, and hedge type (propositional or relational) of the child. Otherwise, these features are null. Likewise, we define *HedgeToken*{Parent,Sibling,DepAncestor}, *HedgeLemma*{Parent,Sibling,DepAncestor}, and *HedgeType*{Parent,Sibling,DepAncestor} if the parent, sibling, or ancestor of the word is classified as a hedge.

- **Sentence features**: based on properties of the sentence containing the current word. If the hedge detector identifies a hedge anywhere in the sentence, *SentenceContainsHedge* is set to true.

5 Experiments and Results

All the experiments reported below use 5-fold cross validation on the 2014 Darpa DEFT Committed Belief Corpus (Release No. LDC2014E55). The documents in this corpus are from English discussion forum data. We compare the performance of the system using (a) no hedge features (b) hedge features obtained using the dictionary-based tagger, and (c) hedge features obtained using the rule-based tagger. Results are shown in Table 3. Note that our baseline results differ slightly from the System C results presented in Prabhakaran et al. (2015) because the training/evaluation datasets used are different. Additionally, our baseline uses no hedge features while System C uses simple word-based hedge features based on an earlier version of our hedging dictionary.

As we might expect, hedge features are most significant in detecting instances of reported belief and non-committed belief. Since these represent only a small portion of the full corpus, the effect on the overall performance is not large. However it is still significant. Using dictionary-based hedge features, we see an increase of 1.82 in the f-measure for ROB as compared to the baseline, from 23.29 to 25.11, and an increase of 2.29 for NCB, from 23.66 to 25.95. The overall f-score increases 0.43, from 67.52 to 69.95. Using rule-based hedge features, the increase compared to the baseline is more significant. For ROB, the f-score shows an increase of 4.14, from 23.29 to 27.43. For NCB, the f-score increases 6.77, from 23.66 to 30.43. The overall increase in the f-score using the rule-based hedge features is 0.55, from 67.52 to 68.07.

Tag (count)	**Precision**	**Recall**	**F-measure**
ROB (256)	28.02	19.92	23.29
NCB (193)	44.93	16.06	23.66
NA (2762)	77.49	56.34	65.24
CB (4299)	69.80	74.78	72.21
Overall	70.69	64.62	67.52

(a)

Tag (count)	**Precision**	**Recall**	**F-measure**
ROB (256)	30.22	21.48	25.11
NCB (193)	49.28	17.62	25.95
NA (2762)	77.69	56.73	65.58
CB (4299)	70.27	75.04	72.58
Overall	71.18	65.01	67.95

(b)

Tag (count)	**Precision**	**Recall**	**F-measure**
ROB (256)	31.63	24.22	27.43
NCB (193)	50.60	21.76	30.43
NA (2762)	77.89	56.52	65.51
CB (4299)	70.58	74.95	72.70
Overall	71.36	65.07	68.07

(c)

Table 3: Belief results using (a) no hedge detection, (b) dictionary-based hedge detection, and (c) rule-based hedge detection.

6 Summary and Future Work

We have shown that hedge detection can improve the performance of a committed belief tagger, particularly in identifying instances of reported belief and non-committed belief. Using hedge features based on simple dictionary-lookup improves performance compared to the baseline; the addition of manually constructed rules improves performance further. While these results are promising, there are limits to the rule-based approach we have presented. In many cases, it is not straightforward to define a simple rule disambiguating hedge from non-hedge use.

To address these issues, we use Amazon Mechanical Turk to construct a corpus of forum posts labeled with hedge information. Although other labeled corpora exist, these are in other domains and may not apply to the forum data we are using. After finding potential hedges in the forum posts from the 2014 Deft Committed Belief Corpora

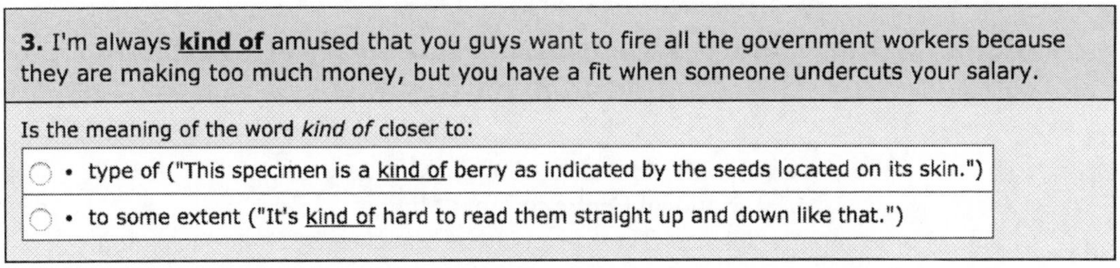

Figure 1: Example of AMT word disambiguation task.

(Release No. LDC2014E55, LDC2014E106, and LDC2014E125), we present each potential hedge to turkers as a highlighted word or phrase within a sentence. Rather than asking turkers to label the word as a hedge or not, we show the definitions of hedging and non-hedging uses of the term from our hedge dictionary (see Section 3 and ask workers which most closely matches the meaning of the word. Figure 1 shows an example for the phrase *kind of*. In future work, we will use this corpus to evaluate the rule-based hedge detector and to train machine learning classifiers directly from the labeled corpus. By this means, we hope to continue to improve the performance of the committed belief tagger as well.

Acknowledgments

This paper is based upon work supported by the DARPA DEFT program. The views expressed here are those of the author(s) and do not reflect the official policy or position of the Department of Defense or the U.S. Government.

References

David Clausen. 2010. Hedgehunter: A system for hedge detection and uncertainty classification. In *Proceedings of the Fourteenth Conference on Computational Natural Language Learning*, pages 120–125, Uppsala, Sweden. Association for Computational Linguistics.

Richárd Farkas, Veronika Vincze, György Móra, János Csirik, and György Szarvas. 2010. The conll-2010 shared task: Learning to detect hedges and their scope in natural language text. In *Proceedings of the Fourteenth Conference on Computational Natural Language Learning*, pages 1–12, Uppsala, Sweden. Association for Computational Linguistics.

Vinodkumar Prabhakaran, Tomas By, Julia Hirschberg, Owen Rambow, Samira Shaikh, Tomek Strzalkowski, Jennifer Tracey, Michael Arrigo, Rupayan Basu, Micah Clark, Adam Dalton, Mona Diab, Louise Guthrie, Anna Prokofieva, Stephanie Strassel, Gregory Werner, Yorick Wilks, and Janyce Wiebe. 2015. A new dataset and evaluation for belief/factuality. In *Proceedings of the Fourth Joint Conference on Lexical and Computational Semantics*, pages 82–91, Denver, Colorado. Association for Computational Linguistics.

Vinodkumar Prabhakaran, Owen Rambow, and Mona Diab. 2010. Automatic committed belief tagging. In *Coling 2010: Posters*, pages 1014–1022, Beijing, China. Coling 2010 Organizing Committee.

Anna Prokofieva and Julia Hirschberg. 2014. Hedging and speaker commitment. In *5th Intl. Workshop on Emotion, Social Signals, Sentiment & Linked Open Data*, Reykjavik, Iceland.

Buzhou Tang, Xiaolong Wang, Xuan Wang, Bo Yuan, and Shixi Fan. 2010. A cascade method for detecting hedges and their scope in natural language text. In *Proceedings of the Fourteenth Conference on Computational Natural Language Learning*, pages 13–17, Uppsala, Sweden. Association for Computational Linguistics.

Erik Velldal. 2011. Predicting speculation: a simple disambiguation approach to hedge detection in biomedical literature. *Journal of Biomedical Semantics*, 2(5):S7.

Veronika Vincze, György Szarvas, Richárd Farkas, György Móra, and János Csirik. 2008. The bioscope corpus: biomedical texts annotated for uncertainty, negation and their scopes. *BMC Bioinformatics*, 9(11):S9.

Andreas Vlachos and Mark Craven. 2010. Detecting speculative language using syntactic dependencies and logistic regression. In *Proceedings of the Fourteenth Conference on Computational Natural Language Learning*, pages 18–25, Uppsala, Sweden. Association for Computational Linguistics.

Paths for Uncertainty: Exploring the Intricacies of Uncertainty Identification for News

Chrysoula Zerva, **Sophia Ananiadou**
National Centre for Text Mining
School of Computer Science, The University of Manchester, United Kingdom
{chrysoula.zerva, sophia.ananiadou}@manchester.ac.uk

Abstract

Currently, news articles are produced, shared and consumed at an extremely rapid rate. Although their quantity is increasing, at the same time, their quality and trustworthiness is becoming fuzzier. Hence, it is important not only to automate information extraction but also to quantify the certainty of this information. Automated identification of expressions that affect certainty has been studied both in the scientific and newswire domains, but performance is considerably higher in tasks focusing on scientific text. We compare the differences in the definition and expression of uncertainty between a scientific domain, i.e., biomedicine, and newswire. We delve into the different aspects that affect the certainty of an extracted event in a news article and examine whether they can be easily identified by techniques already validated in the biomedical domain. Finally, we present a comparison of the syntactic and lexical differences between the the expression of certainty in the biomedical and newswire domains, using two annotated corpora.

1 Introduction

The increasing amount of data readily available in digital form across various domains presents challenges for both researchers and the general public. Although this has greatly improved access to data and dissemination of knowledge, it is becoming increasingly difficult to quickly identify a piece of information that is pertinent to our needs among the vast amounts of data, as well as to assess its certainty and credibility. Advances in information extraction methods and in particular *event* extraction tasks (McClosky et al., 2011; Nguyen et al., 2016; Cao et al., 2016), capture complex information structures to that can capture n-ary relations between entities, and better represent facts and statements made by authors.

While being able to extract rich information in a structured manner is important, not all extracted information is equally trustworthy. It is thus necessary to apply measures of confidence that will allow us to assess the credibility of events mined from different documents. Such measures may take into account different factors affecting our confidence in a specific event, such as the reliability of the source (Lucassen and Schraagen, 2010), the timeliness of the event (Pustejovsky, 2017), the performance of the event extraction tool etc. Along with such "external" factors affecting our trust in the event, another important aspect is how certainty is expressed in the context of the event by the author, since not all information mentioned in text is expressed with equal certainty. Some events are explicitly identified as speculations, as hypothetical situations, as disputed allegations, as conditional facts, and so on. Thus, it is important to complement event extraction methods with identification of such textual phenomena, in order to enrich extracted events with an attribute of certainty.

Identification of textual uncertainty and hedging is a mature research topic, with an emphasis on the scientific domain (Hyland, 1998). Methods to detect certainty and related types of information are widely applied in the field of biomedical text mining to assess the veracity of information, and the problem is approached both in terms of framing certainty and annotating corpora accordingly, and by applying machine learning techniques for the automated identification of uncertain statements and events (Kilicoglu et al., 2017; Malhotra et al., 2013). In the news domain, while machine learning techniques have been used to mine sentiment, subjectivity etc, efforts concerned with (un)certainty identification have focussed mostly on the provision of classification framework for uncertainty (Rubin, 2010) or its combination with polarity to determine event factuality (Sauri and Pustejovsky, 2007). However, there has been less emphasis on applications that focus on automatically recognising uncertainty,

Proceedings of the Workshop on Computational Semantics beyond Events and Roles (SemBEaR-2018), pages 6–20
New Orleans, Louisiana, June 5, 2018. ©2017 Association for Computational Linguistics

especially in relation to events. Moreover, early attempts at automated identification of uncertainty cues (weasels) in both the general and biomedical domains showed more than 0.30 difference in F-score between the two domains (0.50 for Wikipedia versus 0.87 for Bio (Tang et al., 2010)), thus illustrating the challenges of uncertainty identification in the general language domain.

Newswire text can prove more problematic in terms of uncertainty identification, since news stories tend to be reported in a subjective manner (Godbole et al., 2007; Vis, 2011) and allow for less strict use of language, while the truth value of reported events greatly depends on the time and context in which an article is written. As uncertainty identification is affected by various textual phenomena which are challenging to contextualise (metaphorical speech, colloquial expressions, etc), methods that identify event uncertainty from context are becoming increasingly crucial. The widespread use of the term "fake news" in recent years highlights the need to distinguish valuable and reliable facts, especially when it comes to automated information extraction. While detection of fake news is an involved process requiring more in depth discourse and stance analysis (Thorne et al., 2017), identifying certainty of extracted events is an important parameter towards the assessment of credibility of such events. The availability of an increasing number of resources annotated with news events and concepts related to uncertainty provide good opportunities to apply and adapt uncertainty identification techniques that are focussed on news articles.

In this work, we present our efforts on adapting uncertainty event extraction techniques developed for biomedical text, to allow them to be applied to newswire text. We use two corpora annotated with events and meta-knowledge (different types of interpretative information within a sentence that can affect an event (Thompson et al., 2011)) to analyse the differences between the two domains and we discuss the challenges that arise. We evaluate a hybrid machine learning approach to the identification of different uncertainty aspects (see Section 3.2.1) and propose ways of improving and customising uncertainty identification for newswire.

2 Related Work

In this section, we provide an overview of related work on uncertainty in both the scientific and newswire domains. We examine different classification frameworks of uncertainty and related concepts, the availability of annotations and existing classification systems used in each field.

The means of conveying uncertainty have long been studied by linguists, using a range of different terminology. Palmer (2001) introduced the term *epistemic modality* to refer to the degree of commitment to the truth of a proposition. The term continues to be used, especially for scientific text (De Waard and Maat, 2012; Vold, 2006) along with other related terms, such as *factuality*, which combines the notions of uncertainty and polarity (Saurí, 2017), *veracity* and *evidentiality* (Cornillie, 2009; Davis et al., 2007). The use of hedge words and their impact on the certainty of statements has also been studied extensively both in the scientific (Morante et al., 2010) and generic domain (Ganter and Strube, 2009). As computational technologies have evolved, there has been an increasing interest in the implications of textual uncertainty and the way it is expressed, resulting in a wide range of classification frameworks and annotation efforts.

In the scientific domain, Light (2004) studied uncertainty in biomedical papers, classifying expressions as denoting high or low certainty. Medlock and Briscoe (2007) further expanded the categorisation to incorporate the cases of admission of lack of knowledge, relays of hypotheses from others, speculative questions and hypotheses (investigation). More recently, Chen (2018) proposed a wider definition of uncertainty that covers phenomena of citation distortion, contradictions and claim inconsistencies, and also presented a method based on word embeddings for expanding a small seed list of cues to generate rich resources for uncertainty identification.

The aforementioned concepts have also been annotated in corpora at different levels of granularity. The BioScope corpus (Vincze et al., 2008), as well the biomedical part of the CoNLL 2010 task (Farkas et al., 2010) contain annotations of speculation and negation cues and their scope within the sentence. The BioNLP Shared Task corpora (Kim et al., 2009, 2011; Nédellec et al., 2013) also contain speculation and negation annotations, marked-up as attributes of events. The GENIA-MK corpus (Thompson et al., 2011) also contains event-level attribute annotations, but covering more meta-knowledge aspects, including *certainty level*, *polarity* and *knowledge type* (see Section 3.2.1). Various models for the automated identification of the types of information annotated in the aforementioned corpora have been developed , with the best performing methods using a combination of rules and machine learning approaches. Overall, performance is highest for sentence-based annotations, with recent work reaching an F-score of 0.97 on BioScope (Kilicoglu et al., 2017), while on the event-level annotations of GENIA-MK, the best reported F-score surpasses 0.80 for the 3-level certainty classification problem (Miwa et al., 2012) and 0.88 for the binary problem (Zerva et al., 2017).

Bridging definitions of uncertainty across different domains, Szarvas (2012) proposes a hierarchical categorisation which distinguishes between two main classes: hypothetical and epistemic uncertainty. Vincze (2013), attempts a different categorization, looking at discourse-level uncertainty and related phenomena as they appear in text in the generic domain (Wikipedia). They identify three different types of uncertainty; weasels (relevant but insufficiently specified arguments), hedges and peacocks (exaggerated, subjective statements).

On work dealing with newspaper articles, subjectivity is identified as a further phenomenon (along with hedging and speculation) that is inextricably related to the expression of uncertainty (Rubin, 2007; Morante and Daelemans, 2009). Moreover, Rubin (2010) proposes a four-dimensional classification of certainty, also pointing out the aspect of timeliness and focus (abstract versus factual information). Their proposed annotation schema was applied to a small corpus of 82 documents. In terms of further resources, FactBank (Saurí and Pustejovsky, 2009) is a small corpus consisting of texts from the newswire domain annotated with events, accompanied with their factuality value (a combination of certainty level and polarity) judged from the viewpoint of their sources. The MPQA corpus (Cardie et al., 2003) elaborates on the issue of subjectivity and combines it with polarity markers to classify different opinions. The ACE 2005 corpus (Walker et al., 2006) contains events from news texts that are annotated with meta-knowledge attributes, among which *modality* and *genericity*. Subsequently, the meta-knowledge annotations were extended to include among others the aspect of *subjectivity* (see Section 3.2.1). More recently, there has been significant work in assessing factuality and credibility of news articles, as part of the fake-news challenge (FNC-I) that focusses on detection of stance.

In comparison to the scientific domain, there have been relatively fewer attempts to automatically identify uncertainty in news text, apart from the classification of particular aspects that embody uncertainty, such as subjectivity (Wilson, 2008). The most significant work is the wikipedia related task of CoNLL 2010, which concerned weasel cue detection. The best performing systems at the time compared poorly to the results in the biomedical field but more recently Jean (2016) proposed a probabilistic model that achieved an F-score of 55.7, showing a promising degree of improvement. Even more encouragingly, there have recently been important efforts on the classification of factuality values based on FactBank and related factuality corpora (UW, MEANTIME), showing great improvements in their predictions (Stanovsky et al., 2017; Lee et al., 2015) compared to earlier attempts (Prabhakaran et al., 2010). Such efforts motivate our interest in studying the detection of uncertainty in the newswire domain.

3 Methods

In this section, we provide a definition of the problem we aim to tackle, as well as definitions of terms that we use subsequently. We also describe the datasets and resources that we have used, and we present the methods and technical details used for the experiments and analysis in Section 4.

3.1 Event Definition

In both the GENIA-MK and the ACE-MK corpora, the definition of events shares some core properties. An event consists necessarily of one trigger entity and usually one or more participant NEs (arguments) that are linked to the trigger. The trigger entity determines the type of the event, and is usually one word (can be verb, noun or adjective) that describes the event. Similarly, the relation between the trigger and each argument determines argument's role. Examples of events from the two domains are presented in Figure 1.

3.2 Uncertainty Identification Task

As described in the previous section, uncertainty can be interpreted in different ways. In this work, we cast uncertainty identification as the task of identifying textual information (cues) that render the truth of a specific *event* uncertain. Hence,

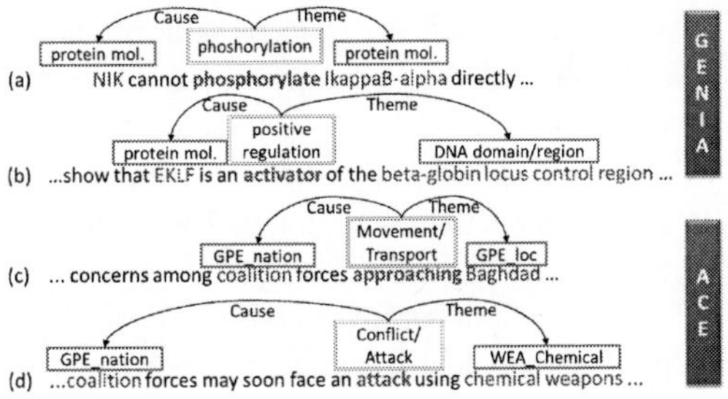

Figure 1: Event examples extracted from GENIA-MK (a-b) and ACE-MK (c-d).

uncertainty is treated as an attribute of an event, rather than an attribute of a sentence or clause. This is because it has been shown that a given unit of text may contain more than one event, each with a potentially different level of uncertainty (Saurí and Pustejovsky, 2009; Thompson et al., 2017). We limit the discovery of uncertainty cues to those occurring in same sentence as the event in question, following the annotations of the two corpora.

We cast uncertainty identification as a binary classification task, where an event can either be *certain* or *uncertain*. Our decision was motivated by the findings of Rubin (2007) who showed that a finer grained classification of uncertainty (5 levels) resulted in unacceptably low levels of inter-annotator agreement.

We treat uncertainty of an event as an attribute that can be affected by various factors (modality, hypothesis, subjectivity etc), that are already annotated in existing corpora. Hence, we want to take advantage of existing corpora annotations, and examine how such annotations relate to uncertainty, either individually or combined. We examine the performance and robustness of automated uncertainty identification method developed in (Zerva et al., 2017) based on different combinations of meta-knowledge dimensions to draw our conclusions, acknowledging that (as discussed in Section 2) for different domains there can be different dimensions affecting uncertainty. In the following section, we describe the datasets as well the meta-knowledge annotations that we consider to be related to uncertainty identification in the biomedical and newswire domains.

3.2.1 Datasets and Uncertainty

We focus our analysis for the newswire domain on the recent annotations of the ACE 2005 corpus (Walker et al., 2006) (English version). The corpus was originally annotated with named entities (NEs), events, as well as some meta-knowledge information and has been subsequently enriched with additional meta-knowledge annotations (Thompson et al., 2017). We refer to the meta-knowledge annotated version of the corpus as ACE-MK [1]. The corpus comprises of 600 news articles originating from various sources, and contains annotations for 5349 events. The ACE-MK meta-knowledge annotation scheme, includes 6 meta-knowledge attributes, of which four (4) were present in the original 2005 annotated corpus and the rest were introduced in the 2017 annotation enrichment effort (the latter are marked with an asterisk in the enumeration that follows). The respective cues for each type were annotated whenever present within a sentence.

1. Subjectivity (*) towards the event by the source. Can be Positive, Negative, Neutral or Multi-valued (two or more sources expressing opposite sentiments for the same event).

2. Source (*), that can be Author, Involved (attributed to a specified source, somehow involved with the event) or Third-Party.

3. Modality, that can have four possible values; Asserted, Speculated, Presupposed(*) and Other

4. Polarity, that can be either Positive or Negative.

5. Tense, that can be Past, Present, Future or Unspecified.

6. Genericity, that can either be Specific (event referring to a specific occurrence) or Generic.

As discussed in Section 2, various concepts, such as modality, subjectivity, genericity and timeliness have been linked to uncertainty in the newswire domain. In fact, most of the aforementioned event attributes annotated in ACE-MK could affect event certainty. In this work, we focus on the dimensions of *Modality*, *Genericity* and *Subjectivity*. (Saurí and Pustejovsky, 2009) Considering these three different attributes as well as their combination as uncertainty indicators, we generate four different test-sets, each corresponding to a different uncertainty definition:

[1] The ACE-MK corpus annotations and guidelines are available at `http://www.nactem.ac.uk/ace-mk/`.

1. M: uncertainty corresponds only to *Modality*, and only *Asserted* events are equivalent to *Certain*. Based on descriptions in (Baker et al., 2014; Szarvas et al., 2012).

2. G: uncertainty corresponds only to *Genericity*, and only *Specific* events are equivalent to *Certain*. We thus claim that that generic, more vague events lack certainty, inspired by the distinction between abstract and specific statements in (Rubin, 2010).

3. S: uncertainty corresponds only to *Subjectivity*, and only *Neutral* events are equivalent to *Certain*. Based on (Wiebe and Riloff, 2005) which has shown that positive or negative bias can affect the certainty of an event. *Multi-valued* instances are treated as *Uncertain* since contradictory assertions have also been linked to uncertainty (Alamri, 2016).

4. MGS : uncertainty corresponds to the union of the above; only an event that is *Asserted*, *Neutral* and *Specific* is considered *Certain*.

In both corpora, the annotations of all meta-knowledge dimensions are on the event level (the values of each event annotated separately). The evidence, if it can be attributed to one or more words in the same sentence as the event, is annotated as a cue, for the dimension annotated, and linked to the event(s) that it affects. In Figure 2 (a-b) we demonstrate one example from each corpus where the cue affects only one of the events in a sentence. While in both corpora for most dimensions investigated the cues are word sequences different than the trigger of the event, for Subjectivity, we have cases where the trigger is also acting like a Subjectivity cue. This is because based on the definition of Subjectivity for ACE-MK, biased attitude expressed in text denotes subjectivity (including expressions of intention, command, fear, hope, condemn etc). Example (c) in Figure 2 demonstrates such a case.

(a)	It was **not clear** whether any Iraqi leader had been *killed* in the *airstrike* targeting Saddam in an upscale Baghdad neighborhood.	Modality: Speculated
(b)	To **investigate** the *effect* of NAC on the *induction phase* of T cell responses	KT: Investigation
(c)	... the HMOs and the nursing home chains have ***poured*** into members of Congress' coffers	Subjectivity: Negative

Figure 2: Examples of cue annotations. Cues are in bold-red while events in green-italic. Events that are affected by the highlighted cue are underlined in each sentence.

We train and test separate classifiers for each case and discuss their performance and the implication on the predictability of uncertainty.

We should note that *Polarity* has been identified as a dimension that is orthogonal to uncertainty (Saurí and Pustejovsky, 2009) and thus we choose not to include it in our investigation, although both corpora contain such annotations. In future work, we would like to further investigate the combination of certainty and polarity and maybe expand our analysis on the FactBank corpus. It would also be interesting, as future work, to expand our experiments and investigate whether *Tense* could also be used to account for the timeliness aspect, or whether *Source* could help to identify weaselling phenomena, thus expanding the coverage of uncertainty. For an efficient accounting of these two dimensions in future work, we would like to include additional resources such as timeliness or citation analysis components.

Apart from comparing performance among the different uncertainty-related definitions described above, we compare our results for ACE-MK with those obtained for a biomedical corpus, GENIA-MK (Kim et al., 2003; Thompson et al., 2011), for binary uncertainty identification using the same hybrid method, as reported in (Zerva et al., 2017).

The GENIA-MK corpus consists of 1000 abstracts extracted from PubMed and annotated with 36,858 events[2]. It has also been annotated with meta-knowledge attributes for each event, and the respective cues. The meta-knowledge attributes for each event include *Certainty Level* (L1, L2, L3), *Polarity* (Positive, Negative), *Manner* (High, Low and Neutral), *Source* (Current, Other) and *Knowledge Type* (Investigation, Observation, Analysis, Method, Fact, Other). Of those, *Certainty Level* L1 and L2 as well as *Knowledge type* of Investigation were treated as uncertainty indicators (denoting an event as *Uncertain*).

3.3 Machine Learning Approach

For the experiments described in Section 4.1 we use a hybrid machine learning approach to classify ACE-MK events as *Certain* or *Uncertain*. We use a Random Forest (RF) classifier (Liaw et al., 2002) and a range of semantic, lexical, syntactic and dependency features. The majority of the lexical features are related to the cue and its sur-

[2]The GENIA-MK annotations are available at: `http://www.nactem.ac.uk/meta-knowledge/`.

face and grammatical properties, while syntactic and dependency features are related to the syntactic dependencies between the cue and the event. Features also include dependency-based rules that capture one and two-hop paths between the cue and an event trigger. Finally, there is an additional set of features related to the semantics of the event itself (event type, arguments). A more detailed description and examples of the features can be found in Appendix A.

The full processing of ACE-MK corpus, including other NLP tasks such as sentence splitting, tokenisation etc, was performed using Argo platform, a web-based, graphical workbench that facilitates the construction and execution of modular text mining workflows (Batista-Navarro et al., 2017). For the implementation of the RF classifier, dedicated components were implemented using the WEKA API (Frank et al., 2004). We used 10-fold cross-validation to evaluate and compare the performance of different generated models. Since some of the features are sentence and/or document based, we avoided the automated 10-fold cross validation of the WEKA API, and instead modified the random fold generation so that no document would be split over several folds, thus ensuring the models were not biased or overfitted to specific documents.

3.4 WordNet-based Analysis

In order to interpret the differences in the performance of our models between the GENIA-MK and the ACE-MK, we compared the lexical and semantic properties of the cues in each corpus. For this purpose, we used WordNet (Miller, 1995) version 3.0 to examine the synsets and relations between uncertainty cues, the generated word graphs and the distributions of cues per synset. To process cues against information contained within WordNet, the JWI API (Finlayson, 2014) was used.

In order to study the links between cues, we consider WordNet as a multi-graph where each word is a node, and all potential relations between two words constitute an edge. The types of relations are used as edge attributes. To generate the graph from each corpus, we start with the lemmatised cues and iteratively expand the graph using a set of available relations between words as well as synsets until there are no other nodes to visit. We use all relations available in WordNet between synsets and words, but we exclude expansion for some senses that are semantically irrelevant to all potential cues, as described in Appendix B.

The analysis and visualisation of the graphs was performed using Gephi (Bastian et al., 2009).

4 Results and Discussion

4.1 Automated Classification of Uncertainty

As a first step, we used the set of cues extracted from GENIA-MK for the generation of all features in the cue and dependency related feature sets. We then trained and evaluated the performance of the trained models on each of the test sets of the ACE-MK corpus, as shown in the top three rows of Table 1. The results show that the classifier trained with GENIA-MK cues does not achieve particularly high performance for any of the three cases of uncertainty, or for their combination. We subsequently proceeded to replace the GENIA-MK cues with the ones extracted from the ACE-MK corpus, and repeated the experiments, as shown in the bottom three rows Table 1.

When using ACE-MK cues, F-score increases significantly ($p < 0.01$) for all different test sets. This is mostly due to the consistent improvement in recall for all test sets (in terms of precision, it is only the case of *Modality* that the ACE-MK cues outperform the GENIA-MK cues). This result confirms the domain dependence of uncertainty expressions and stresses the need of domain specific approaches, to achieve higher performance.

	M	G	S	MGS	Cues
Precision	0.53	0.27	0.40	0.61	
Recall	0.55	0.62	0.46	0.69	GEN
F-score	0.54	0.38	0.34	0.65	
Precision	0.57	0.26	0.40	**0.69**	
Recall	0.69	0.67	0.63	**0.74**	ACE
F-score	0.62	0.37	0.49	**0.71**	

Table 1: Performance of uncertainty identification on each uncertainty test-case using GENIA-MK (GEN) and ACE-MK (ACE) cues.

	GENIA-MK cues	ACE-MK cues
Precision	0.94	0.82
Recall	0.83	0.86
F-score	0.88	0.84

Table 2: Performance for uncertainty identification on GENIA-MK corpus using different cues.

More interestingly however, we notice that even when using ACE-MK cues, the performance we obtain is significantly lower compared to the performance obtained when the same method is applied to the GENIA-MK corpus. Indeed we see in Table 2 that on GENIA-MK even when using cues extracted from ACE-MK, performance is significantly higher for all metrics (Zerva et al., 2017).

Genericity seems to be the hardest attribute to distinguish, especially in terms of precision. This can be explained through an examination of the training data, which reveals that there are very few Generic event instances that are linked to a Genericity cue. Thus, while there is a sufficient number of training instances for Generic events (1132 Generic versus 4217 Specific) strong feature vectors can only be produced for a few of them. The classifier also seems to be having difficulties in predicting *Subjectivity*, but for different reasons. Looking more closely at the results for *Subjectivity*, we discovered that one issue relates to Multi-valued test cases, which are particularly complex since they often involve the existence of more than one Subjectivity cue linked with the event, and at the same time they are significantly under-sampled (18 instances). Moreover, Subjectivity cues seem to involve more nouns and longer, often colloquial expressions compared to other dimensions.

Further enhancement of the machine learning approach and feature engineering could try to address such issues, in order to better identify *Subjectivity* and *Genericity* dimensions. A possible future direction would be to enhance current vectors methods that can account for positive or negative bias of nouns, or other methods borrowed by work on subjectivity. Coupled with a training corpus containing more positive instances, such methods could help drawing further conclusions.

In the last column of Table 1 we present the performance of the models trained on the combined dimensions. By combining the meta-knowledge dimensions into one uncertainty identification task, we can see that we get improved performance, compared to the individual tasks. This provides an indication that relationships exist between these different dimensions in the context of detecting uncertainty. Still, as mentioned earlier, we notice that for all possible combinations, performance is lower compared to results reported for biomedical corpora using the same machine learning approach, even when we use cues extracted from the same corpus. This difference in score, even in the case of Modality, much like the one seen in the work of (Tang et al., 2010) for the CoNLL datasets, provides motivation to look more closely into the differences between the means of expressing uncertainty in the two different domains. In the next section, we attempt to interpret this difference in performance, explore why the cue and dependency based features used might be less effective for the newswire domain, and what could be done to remedy this.

4.2 Comparison of the Properties of Uncertainty Cues Between Corpora

4.2.1 Dependency-based Comparison

As mentioned in Section 3.2.1 the machine learning classifiers used in this work, are heavily dependent on features related to the dependencies between potential uncertainty cues and the triggers of events. For the extraction of dependency paths we use a dependency parser in order to extract the dependency relations for each sentence of the corpus. The Enju dependency parser (Miyao et al., 2008) was used for both corpora, with models trained on biomedical and newswire data for GENIA-MK and ACE-MK respectively.

We then treat the dependencies as a directed graph and examine the shortest paths between annotated cues and event triggers as shown in the example of Figure 4. In case of multi-word cues or multi-word events we consider the shortest possible path between any word of the cue and any word of the trigger. The comparison of dependency path lengths for the two corpora can be seen in Figure 3.

It is clear from the distribution that the dependency paths for the GENIA-MK corpus (gray-

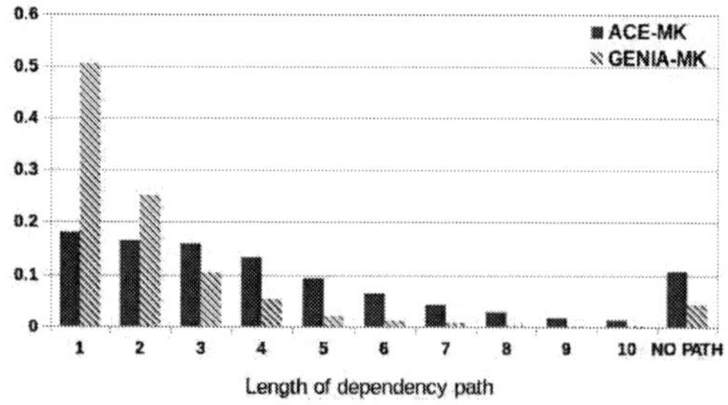

Figure 3: Histogram of length distribution for shortest dependency paths between uncertainty cues and triggers for ACE-MK and GENIA-MK.

striped bars) follows a long-tail pattern, with more than 50% of the cues being directly linked to the trigger and more than 85% being at a distance of three or less dependency links. On the contrary for ACE-MK corpus we have a more evenly spread distribution of dependency paths, since to contain 85% of the cases we need to reach dependency paths of length 7. Looking at the last bar of the histogram, which accounts for paths longer than ten (10) hops or non-existent paths, we note that the percentage of such cases is double for ACE-MK compared to GENIA-MK.

This difference in the dependency path distribution, could explain why features based on dependency paths as well as dependency rules are not as efficient for newswire documents. Indeed, analysis of feature informativeness (using Mutual Information measures (Battiti, 1994)) for the two corpora further supports these observations. In the 30 top scoring features for GENIA-MK, 19 are dependency features (14 of them dependency rules) versus only 5 dependency features for ACE-MK (and only 1 dependency rule). These observations reveal a potential higher complexity in the sentence syntax and language structure in newswire texts as opposed to scientific texts. For example, in ACE-MK we observe more occurrences of event triggers being nouns that are not close to the main verb (and surrounding modals) and of cues indicating uncertainty (especially Subjectivity) found in a different sub-phrase than the event (see Figure 3). There are also some wrongly structured sentences where the dependency paths are distorted due to problematic syntax.

This difference may occur as a result of the

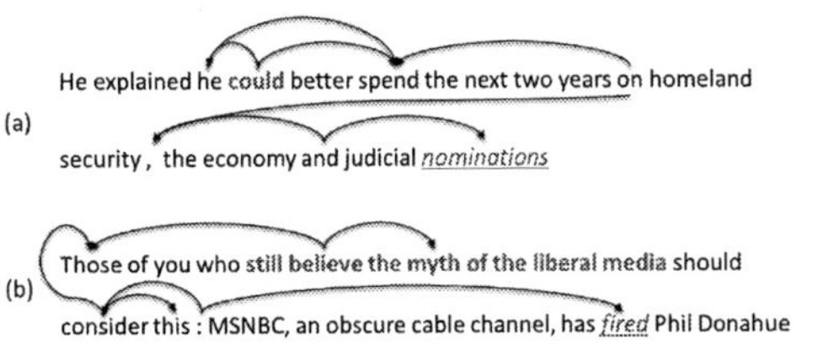

Figure 4: Dependency paths between cue (red-bold) and trigger (green-underlined) for ACE-MK. Arrows denote the edges of the dependency graph that participate in the shortest path between cue and trigger. In (a) *could* is a Modality cue, influencing a *Personel_nominates* event. In (b) we have a phrase that is annotated as a Subjectivity cue and the event is *Personnel_end_position*.

greater freedom of expression in news articles as opposed to scientific texts, where language and syntax follow stricter rules, and formal expressions are preferred to colloquial ones. Although it has be shown that even in scientific text, many statements are far from factual assertions, we can expect phenomena of vagueness, weaselling, hedging and speculating to be much more prevalent in news articles compared to scientific ones. It should though be noted that this difference might be further aggravated by the fact that GENIA-MK consists of abstracts, where requirements for precise language are even stricter.

4.2.2 Lexical Comparison

It seems that it is not only in syntax that the two corpora and respective domains differ. By focussing on the lexical and semantic properties of the cue lists in each case, we also found a set of differences at this level. A simple initial observation concerns the differences between the lengths of cues, in terms of the number of words, between the two domains. We can see in Figure 5 that in GENIA-MK, with the exception of some very lengthy outliers, most of the cues are one or two word expressions. In contrast, ACE-MK contains more lengthy uncertainty expressions, including various colloquial expressions, weasels etc.

We also examined the semantic properties of the two cue-lists and generated two WordNet graphs for each corpus as described in Section 3.4. Apart from the sense limitation mentioned before, there was no further attempt to disambiguate cues that belonged to more than one synset. Instead, all possible synsets for each word were added to the graph ending, resulting in a total of 781 synsets covered by the cues for GENIA-MK, compared to 1444 synsets for ACE-MK. Thus the cues in ACE-

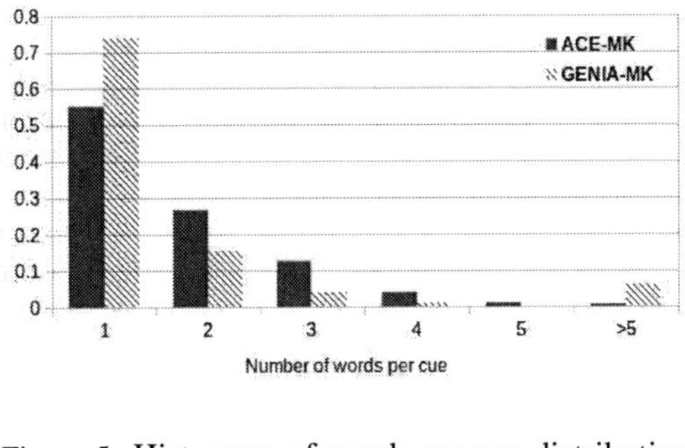

Figure 5: Histogram of words per cue distribution for ACE-MK and GENIA-MK corpora.

MK seems to have a far broader semantic coverage, which means much greater lexical variability and harder to predict cues. To generate the graphs, we use the words in the cue list as seed nodes and then expand them to include all 1-hop neighbors and corresponding edges for each cue. We end up with a graph of 4293 nodes for GENIA-MK and 6123 nodes for ACE-MK.

Looking at the connectivity properties of the two graphs and the number of fully connected components (sub-graphs), we notice that the GENIA-MK graph has only two fully connected sub graphs, versus fifteen (15) for ACE-MK. The difference in sub graphs is another indication supporting the difference in semantic range for the two corpora, although it should be noted that for both corpora 85% of the nodes is contained in the largest sub graph.

We then proceeded to carry out modularity based community detection for the two graphs (Newman, 2006) in order to identify and visualise patterns in the senses of each graph. We focussed on the first 10 largest communities (size calculated on the basis of node count) and their central nodes. To identify central nodes, we ranked nodes using three different centrality measures: betweenness, closeness (Brandes, 2001) and eccentricity (Hage and Harary, 1995) and then used the intersection of the top ranked nodes for each measure. We provide the visualisation of the graphs in Appendix C. As expected, in both graphs the communities are semantically related, and it is easy to see that in some communities the central nodes are related to uncertainty (likelihood, probability etc). Some of the communities evolve around similar concepts, such as ability, probability, communication and investigation, although the concepts are expressed using different terms.

It is important to note that using only 1-hop expansion of the original cues gathered from the two corpora, we were able to generate a graph with semantically meaningful communities. Hence, it would be interesting to further explore the use of WordNet and other semantic graphs as an unsupervised way to expand cue lists and use them on previously unseen data. This could prove particularly useful for domains lacking annotated resources.

5 Conclusion

In this paper we have analysed uncertainty identification in the newswire domain and compared it with the scientific (biomedical) domain both in terms of uncertainty definition and performance of methods. We have explored different meta-knowledge aspects available in newswire corpora, in terms of their relation to uncertainty and the feasibility of their automated identification in text.

We have shown that it is possible to transfer methods similar to the ones employed in the biomedical domain for the automated identification of uncertain events in the news text. However we found that regardless of whether detecting uncertainty is restricted to individual dimensions, or they are treated as a combined task, the performance is significantly lower than the performance obtained by applying the same methods to biomedical articles. To try to understand reasons for this difference, we have analysed the syntactic and lexical properties of textual uncertainty in the newswire domain, and have discovered a number of factors that render the task of uncertainty identification more difficult to tackle in newswire documents. Our analysis has highlighted the role of longer dependencies between cues and events as one of the main issues that complicate the task in newswire articles, along with lengthy cues with increased semantic variability.

We consider this work a promising first step towards a more detailed and fine-tuned approach to uncertainty identification in the newswire domain. As future work, we aim to take advantage of our findings regarding the syntactic and lexical properties that were highlighted above, in order to build more robust classifiers. Moreover, we would like to expand our analysis of uncertainty in the newswire domain using word-embeddings and potentially expand the uncertainty definition in a similar fashion to (Chen et al., 2018). To support this goal, we also intend to experiment with further corpora in the newswire domain.

Efficient uncertainty identification will provide a useful tool for a more meaningful and semantically interpretable information extraction.

Acknowledgments

We would like to thank Mr. Paul Thompson for his invaluable comments that greatly improved the manuscript. This work has been supported by the Engineering and Physical Sciences Research Council [Grant: EP/1038099/1 (CDT)]; and the Biotechnology and Biological Sciences Research Council [Grants: BB/M006891/1 (EMPATHY)].

References

Abdulaziz Alamri. 2016. *The Detection of Contradictory Claims in Biomedical Abstracts*. Ph.D. thesis, University of Sheffield.

Kathryn Baker, Michael Bloodgood, Bonnie J Dorr, Nathaniel W Filardo, Lori Levin, and Christine Piatko. 2014. A modality lexicon and its use in automatic tagging. *arXiv preprint arXiv:1410.4868*.

Mathieu Bastian, Sebastien Heymann, Mathieu Jacomy, et al. 2009. Gephi: an open source software for exploring and manipulating networks. *Icwsm*, 8:361–362.

Riza Batista-Navarro, Nhung TH Nguyen, Axel J Soto, William Ulate, and Sophia Ananiadou. 2017. Argo as a platform for integrating distinct biodiversity analytics tools into workflows for building graph databases. *Proceedings of TDWG*, 1:e20067.

Roberto Battiti. 1994. Using mutual information for selecting features in supervised neural net learning. *IEEE Transactions on neural networks*, 5(4):537–550.

Ulrik Brandes. 2001. A faster algorithm for betweenness centrality. *Journal of mathematical sociology*, 25(2):163–177.

Kai Cao, Xiang Li, and Ralph Grishman. 2016. Leveraging dependency regularization for event extraction. In *FLAIRS Conference*, pages 20–25.

Claire Cardie, Janyce Wiebe, Theresa Wilson, and Diane J Litman. 2003. Combining low-level and summary representations of opinions for multi-perspective question answering. In *New directions in question answering*, pages 20–27.

Chaomei Chen, Min Song, and Go Eun Heo. 2018. A scalable and adaptive method for finding semantically equivalent cue words of uncertainty. *Journal of Informetrics*, 12(1):158–180.

Bert Cornillie. 2009. Evidentiality and epistemic modality: On the close relationship between two different categories. *Functions of language*, 16(1):44–62.

Christopher Davis, Christopher Potts, and Margaret Speas. 2007. The pragmatic values of evidential sentences. In *Semantics and Linguistic Theory*, volume 17, pages 71–88.

Anita De Waard and Henk Pander Maat. 2012. Epistemic modality and knowledge attribution in scientific discourse: A taxonomy of types and overview of features. In *Proceedings of the Workshop on Detecting Structure in Scholarly Discourse*, pages 47–55. Association for Computational Linguistics.

Richárd Farkas, Veronika Vincze, György Móra, János Csirik, and György Szarvas. 2010. The conll-2010 shared task: learning to detect hedges and their scope in natural language text. In *Proceedings of the Fourteenth Conference on Computational Natural Language Learning—Shared Task*, pages 1–12. Association for Computational Linguistics.

Mark Finlayson. 2014. Java libraries for accessing the princeton wordnet: Comparison and evaluation. In *Proceedings of the Seventh Global Wordnet Conference*, pages 78–85.

FNC-I. Fake news challenge. `http://www.fakenewschallenge.org`.

Eibe Frank, Mark Hall, Len Trigg, Geoffrey Holmes, and Ian H Witten. 2004. Data mining in bioinformatics using weka. *Bioinformatics*, 20(15):2479–2481.

Viola Ganter and Michael Strube. 2009. Finding hedges by chasing weasels: Hedge detection using wikipedia tags and shallow linguistic features. In *Proceedings of the ACL-IJCNLP 2009 Conference Short Papers*, pages 173–176. Association for Computational Linguistics.

Namrata Godbole, Manja Srinivasaiah, and Steven Skiena. 2007. Large-scale sentiment analysis for news and blogs. *Icwsm*, 7(21):219–222.

Per Hage and Frank Harary. 1995. Eccentricity and centrality in networks. *Social networks*, 17(1):57–63.

Ken Hyland. 1998. *Hedging in scientific research articles*, volume 54. John Benjamins Publishing.

Pierre-Antoine Jean, Sébastien Harispe, Sylvie Ranwez, Patrice Bellot, and Jacky Montmain. 2016. Uncertainty detection in natural language: A probabilistic model. In *Proceedings of the 6th International Conference on Web Intelligence, Mining and Semantics*, page 10. ACM.

Halil Kilicoglu, Graciela Rosemblat, and Thomas C Rindflesch. 2017. Assigning factuality values to semantic relations extracted from biomedical research literature. *PloS one*, 12(7):e0179926.

J-D Kim, Tomoko Ohta, Yuka Tateisi, and Junichi Tsujii. 2003. Genia corpusa semantically annotated corpus for bio-textmining. *Bioinformatics*, 19(suppl_1):i180–i182.

Jin-Dong Kim, Tomoko Ohta, Sampo Pyysalo, Yoshinobu Kano, and Jun'ichi Tsujii. 2009. Overview of bionlp'09 shared task on event extraction. In *Proceedings of the Workshop on Current Trends in Biomedical Natural Language Processing: Shared Task*, pages 1–9. Association for Computational Linguistics.

Jin-Dong Kim, Sampo Pyysalo, Tomoko Ohta, Robert Bossy, Ngan Nguyen, and Jun'ichi Tsujii. 2011. Overview of bionlp shared task 2011. In *Proceedings of the BioNLP shared task 2011 workshop*, pages 1–6. Association for Computational Linguistics.

Kenton Lee, Yoav Artzi, Yejin Choi, and Luke Zettlemoyer. 2015. Event detection and factuality assessment with non-expert supervision. In *Proceedings of the 2015 Conference on Empirical Methods in Natural Language Processing*, pages 1643–1648.

Andy Liaw, Matthew Wiener, et al. 2002. Classification and regression by randomforest. *R news*, 2(3):18–22.

Marc Light, Xin Ying Qiu, and Padmini Srinivasan. 2004. The language of bioscience: Facts, speculations, and statements in between. In *HLT-NAACL 2004 Workshop: Linking Biological Literature, Ontologies and Databases*.

Teun Lucassen and Jan Maarten Schraagen. 2010. Trust in wikipedia: how users trust information from an unknown source. In *Proceedings of the 4th workshop on Information credibility*, pages 19–26. ACM.

Ashutosh Malhotra, Erfan Younesi, Harsha Gurulingappa, and Martin Hofmann-Apitius. 2013. hypothesisfinder:a strategy for the detection of speculative statements in scientific text. *PLoS computational biology*, 9(7):e1003117.

David McClosky, Mihai Surdeanu, and Christopher D Manning. 2011. Event extraction as dependency parsing. In *Proceedings of the 49th Annual Meeting of the Association for Computational Linguistics: Human Language Technologies-Volume 1*, pages 1626–1635. Association for Computational Linguistics.

Ben Medlock and Ted Briscoe. 2007. Weakly supervised learning for hedge classification in scientific literature. In *Proceedings of the 45th annual meeting of the association of computational linguistics*, pages 992–999.

George A Miller. 1995. Wordnet: a lexical database for english. *Communications of the ACM*, 38(11):39–41.

Makoto Miwa, Paul Thompson, John McNaught, Douglas B Kell, and Sophia Ananiadou. 2012. Extracting semantically enriched events from biomedical literature. *BMC bioinformatics*, 13(1):108.

Yusuke Miyao, Rune Sætre, Kenji Sagae, Takuya Matsuzaki, and Jun'ichi Tsujii. 2008. Task-oriented evaluation of syntactic parsers and their representations. *Proceedings of ACL-08: HLT*, pages 46–54.

Roser Morante and Walter Daelemans. 2009. Learning the scope of hedge cues in biomedical texts. In *Proceedings of the Workshop on Current Trends in Biomedical Natural Language Processing*, BioNLP '09, pages 28–36, Stroudsburg, PA, USA. Association for Computational Linguistics.

Roser Morante, Vincent Van Asch, and Walter Daelemans. 2010. Memory-based resolution of in-sentence scopes of hedge cues. In *Proceedings of the Fourteenth Conference on Computational Natural Language Learning—Shared Task*, pages 40–47. Association for Computational Linguistics.

Claire Nédellec, Robert Bossy, Jin-Dong Kim, Jung-Jae Kim, Tomoko Ohta, Sampo Pyysalo, and Pierre Zweigenbaum. 2013. Overview of bionlp shared task 2013. In *Proceedings of the BioNLP Shared Task 2013 Workshop*, pages 1–7.

Mark EJ Newman. 2006. Modularity and community structure in networks. *Proceedings of the national academy of sciences*, 103(23):8577–8582.

Thien Huu Nguyen, Kyunghyun Cho, and Ralph Grishman. 2016. Joint event extraction via recurrent neural networks. In *Proceedings of the 2016 Conference of the North American Chapter of the Association for Computational Linguistics: Human Language Technologies*, pages 300–309.

Frank Robert Palmer. 2001. *Mood and modality*. Cambridge University Press.

Vinodkumar Prabhakaran, Owen Rambow, and Mona Diab. 2010. Automatic committed belief tagging. In *Proceedings of the 23rd International Conference on Computational Linguistics: Posters*, pages 1014–1022. Association for Computational Linguistics.

James Pustejovsky. 2017. Iso-timeml and the annotation of temporal information. In *Handbook of Linguistic Annotation*, pages 941–968. Springer.

Victoria L Rubin. 2007. Stating with certainty or stating with doubt: Intercoder reliability results for manual annotation of epistemically modalized statements. In *Human Language Technologies 2007: The Conference of the North American Chapter of the Association for Computational Linguistics; Companion Volume, Short Papers*, pages 141–144. Association for Computational Linguistics.

Victoria L Rubin. 2010. Epistemic modality: From uncertainty to certainty in the context of information seeking as interactions with texts. *Information Processing & Management*, 46(5):533–540.

Roser Saurí. 2017. Building factbank or how to annotate event factuality one step at a time. In *Handbook of Linguistic Annotation*, pages 905–939. Springer.

Roser Sauri and James Pustejovsky. 2007. Determining modality and factuality for text entailment. In *Semantic Computing, 2007. ICSC 2007. International Conference on*, pages 509–516. IEEE.

Roser Saurí and James Pustejovsky. 2009. Factbank: a corpus annotated with event factuality. *Language resources and evaluation*, 43(3):227.

Gabriel Stanovsky, Judith Eckle-Kohler, Yevgeniy Puzikov, Ido Dagan, and Iryna Gurevych. 2017. Integrating deep linguistic features in factuality prediction over unified datasets. In *Proceedings of the*

55th Annual Meeting of the Association for Computational Linguistics (Volume 2: Short Papers), volume 2, pages 352–357.

György Szarvas, Veronika Vincze, Richárd Farkas, György Móra, and Iryna Gurevych. 2012. Cross-genre and cross-domain detection of semantic uncertainty. *Computational Linguistics*, 38(2):335–367.

Buzhou Tang, Xiaolong Wang, Xuan Wang, Bo Yuan, and Shixi Fan. 2010. A cascade method for detecting hedges and their scope in natural language text. In *Proceedings of the Fourteenth Conference on Computational Natural Language Learning—Shared Task*, pages 13–17. Association for Computational Linguistics.

Paul Thompson, Raheel Nawaz, John McNaught, and Sophia Ananiadou. 2011. Enriching a biomedical event corpus with meta-knowledge annotation. *BMC bioinformatics*, 12(1):393.

Paul Thompson, Raheel Nawaz, John McNaught, and Sophia Ananiadou. 2017. Enriching news events with meta-knowledge information. *Language Resources and Evaluation*, 51(2):409–438.

James Thorne, Mingjie Chen, Giorgos Myrianthous, Jiashu Pu, Xiaoxuan Wang, and Andreas Vlachos. 2017. Fake news stance detection using stacked ensemble of classifiers. In *Proceedings of the 2017 EMNLP Workshop: Natural Language Processing meets Journalism*, pages 80–83.

Veronika Vincze. 2013. Weasels, hedges and peacocks: Discourse-level uncertainty in wikipedia articles.

Veronika Vincze, György Szarvas, Richárd Farkas, György Móra, and János Csirik. 2008. The bioscope corpus: biomedical texts annotated for uncertainty, negation and their scopes. *BMC bioinformatics*, 9(11):S9.

Kirsten Vis. 2011. Subjectivity in news discourse: A corpus linguistic analysis of informalization.

Eva Thue Vold. 2006. Epistemic modality markers in research articles: a cross-linguistic and cross-disciplinary study. *International Journal of Applied Linguistics*, 16(1):61–87.

Christopher Walker, Stephanie Strassel, Julie Medero, and Kazuaki Maeda. 2006. Ace 2005 multilingual training corpus. *Linguistic Data Consortium, Philadelphia*, 57.

Janyce Wiebe and Ellen Riloff. 2005. Creating subjective and objective sentence classifiers from unannotated texts. In *International Conference on Intelligent Text Processing and Computational Linguistics*, pages 486–497. Springer.

Theresa Ann Wilson. 2008. *Fine-grained subjectivity and sentiment analysis: recognizing the intensity, polarity, and attitudes of private states*. University of Pittsburgh.

Chrysoula Zerva, Riza Batista-Navarro, Philip Day, and Sophia Ananiadou. 2017. Using uncertainty to link and rank evidence from biomedical literature for model curation. *Bioinformatics*, 33(23):3784–3792.

A Appendix A: Machine Learning Features

The features presented in Table 3 are used in the models that were generated for all the experiments presented in Section 4 of the main part of the article. The table presents the main feature categories that are extracted for each event (columns 1 and 2), providing a brief description (column 3) and feature type (column 3).

We should note that for the GENIA-MK corpus, features analysis showed that the contribution of lexical features for cues is overshadowed by the dependency rule features, that capture a combination of surface for and dependencies. On the contrary, such features are more informative for the case of ACE-MK uncertainty classification, since as we have shown in the main document, dependency paths are often longer in ACE-MK rendering the dependency rules inefficient in capturing such relations. Moreover, lexical features for events score very high in terms of informativeness in ACE-MK and quite low in GENIA-MK. This could be attributed to the more uniform type of events in GENIA-MK.

We note that for constituency features, command of a word *a* over a word *b*, signifies that in the syntactic tree *a* is the head of a branch that contains *b*. In both corpora, constituency features scored very high in terms of informativeness.

For dependency path rules, features capture the dependency path as a chain of words (lemmatised[3]) and the type of dependency edges between them. For the experiments presented in this work (Section 4.1 of the main part of the article), rules spanning up to 2 consecutive edges were used (1-hop and 2-hop rules). In Figure 6 we present an example of rule extraction from a sentence. The sentence contains one *Modality* cue (would stipulate) and one *Subjectivity* cue (hates). All the paths between any word of each cue and the the event trigger (war) is extracted based on the dependencies (shown above the sentence). Subsequently, all paths that have length equal or shorter than 2 are converted to rules, as shown below the sentence.

[3]Stanford lemmatiser from the CoreNLP toolkit and Enju parser were used for lemmatisation in all features that required lemmas and/or surface forms of words.

In the case of 2-hop rules, the lemma of the word between the cue and the event trigger in the path, is also captured as part of the rule (as shown in the Modality rule of Figure 6).

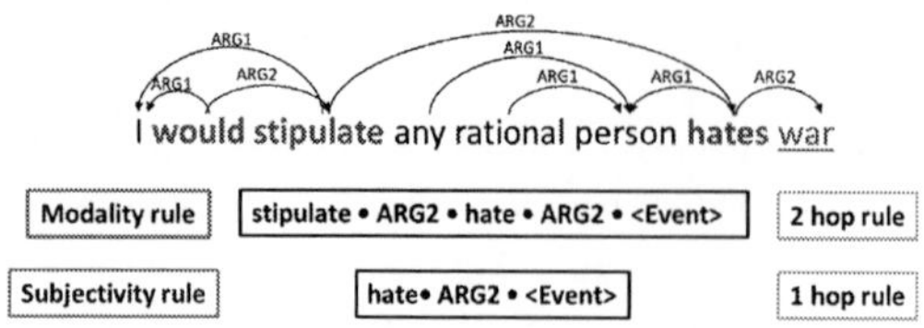

Figure 6: Example of dependency based rule extraction for a phrase extracted from ACE-MK.

B Appendix B: WordNet Senses

When using Wordnet for the graph generation we excluded some of the lexicographic sense groups that are available in WordNet, since they were judged to be too distant to uncertainty expressions (eg referring to specific objects etc). The choice was guided by the description of each sense, in order to avoid senses that do not relate to any of the dimensions of uncertainty described in the main document. By thus excluding senses related to concepts such as food, countries, activities etc we achieve reduced complexity, size and processing time of the resulting graphs. Nevertheless, inclusion of such senses could be interesting to consider in future experiments to see if they can better account for metaphors and colloquial expressions. Alternatively, graphs generated by word embedding approaches could be studied and compared against the WordNet ones.

We list the inclusion/exclusion decision for each of the senses in the Table 4, along with the description of the lexicographer file according to WordNet documentation (`https://wordnet.princeton.edu/documentation/lexnames5wn`).

Cat.	Sub-cat.	Feature	Output
Event	Lexical	Event-trigger surface form	Nom.
		POS tags	Nom.
	Semantic	Event type	Nom.
		Argument type	Nom.
		Argument role	Nom.
	Complexity	Complex/simple	Bin.
Cue	Lexical	Existence of cue	Bin.
		Cue surface form	Nom.
		POS tag of the cue	Nom.
Event & Cue	Relative position	#words between cue and event trigger	Num.
		Position of cue on the left/right of the event trigger	Bin
	Dependency	Direct dependency between cue and trigger	Bin.
		Shortest dependency path length	Num.
		Existence of dependency path rule (see example)	Bin.
		Dependency path rule (see example)	Nom.
	Constituency (syntactic)	Command of cue over trigger	Bin.
		Command of cue over arguments	Bin.

Table 3: Features used for uncertainty identification with the RF classifier. The output column shows the type of the generated feature; *Nom.* denotes nominal features, *Bin.* denotes binary features and *Num.* denotes numeric features.

#	Name	Description	Incl/Excl
0	adj.all	all adjective clusters	Included
1	adj.pert	relational adjectives (pertainyms)	Included
2	adv.all	all adverbs	Included
3	noun.Tops	unique beginner for nouns	Excluded
4	noun.act	nouns denoting acts or actions	Included
5	noun.animal	nouns denoting animals	Excluded
6	noun.artifact	nouns denoting man-made objects	Excluded
7	noun.attribute	nouns denoting attributes of people and objects	Included
8	noun.body	nouns denoting body parts	Excluded
9	noun.cognition	nouns denoting cognitive processes and contents	Included
10	noun.communication	nouns denoting communicative processes and contents	Included
11	noun.event	nouns denoting natural events	Excluded
12	noun.feeling	nouns denoting feelings and emotions	Included
13	noun.food	nouns denoting foods and drinks	Excluded
14	noun.group	nouns denoting groupings of people or objects	Excluded
15	noun.location	nouns denoting spatial position	Excluded
16	noun.motive	nouns denoting goals	Included
17	noun.object	nouns denoting natural objects (not man-made)	Excluded
18	noun.person	nouns denoting people	Excluded
19	noun.phenomenon	nouns denoting natural phenomena	Excluded
20	noun.plant	nouns denoting plants	Excluded
21	noun.possession	nouns denoting possession and transfer of possession	Included
22	noun.process	nouns denoting natural processes	Included
23	noun.quantity	nouns denoting quantities and units of measure	Included
24	noun.relation	nouns denoting relations between people or things or ideas	Included
25	noun.shape	nouns denoting two and three dimensional shapes	Excluded
26	noun.state	nouns denoting stable states of affairs	Included
27	noun.substance	nouns denoting substances	Excluded
28	noun.time	nouns denoting time and temporal relations	Included
29	verb.body	verbs of grooming, dressing and bodily care	Excluded
30	verb.change	verbs of size, temperature change, intensifying, etc.	Included
31	verb.cognition	verbs of thinking, judging, analyzing, doubting	Included
32	verb.communication	verbs of telling, asking, ordering, singing	Included
33	verb.competition	verbs of fighting, athletic activities	Included
34	verb.consumption	verbs of eating and drinking	Excluded
35	verb.contact	verbs of touching, hitting, tying, digging	Excluded
36	verb.creation	verbs of sewing, baking, painting, performing	Excluded
37	verb.emotion	verbs of feeling	Included
38	verb.motion	verbs of walking, flying, swimming	Excluded
39	verb.perception	verbs of seeing, hearing, feeling	Included
40	verb.possession	verbs of buying, selling, owning	Excluded
41	verb.social	verbs of political and social activities and events	Included
42	verb.stative	verbs of being, having, spatial relations	Included
43	verb.weather	verbs of raining, snowing, thawing, thundering	Excluded
44	adj.ppl	participial adjectives	Included

Table 4: WordNet sense description and eligibility for graph generation.

C Appendix C: WordNet Graphs

We present below the ACE-MK and GENIA-MK graphs that are described in Section 4.2.2 of the main part of the article. Different colors signify different communities as identified by community detection based on the modularity index of nodes. We visualise only the ten largest (in terms of the participating nodes) communities). We also visualise the top scoring words (regarded as representatives of each community) for the combination of Closeness, Betweenness and Eccentricity metrics.

In Figure 7 we observe the graph for the ACE-MK corpus while in Figure 8 the one for GENIA-MK.

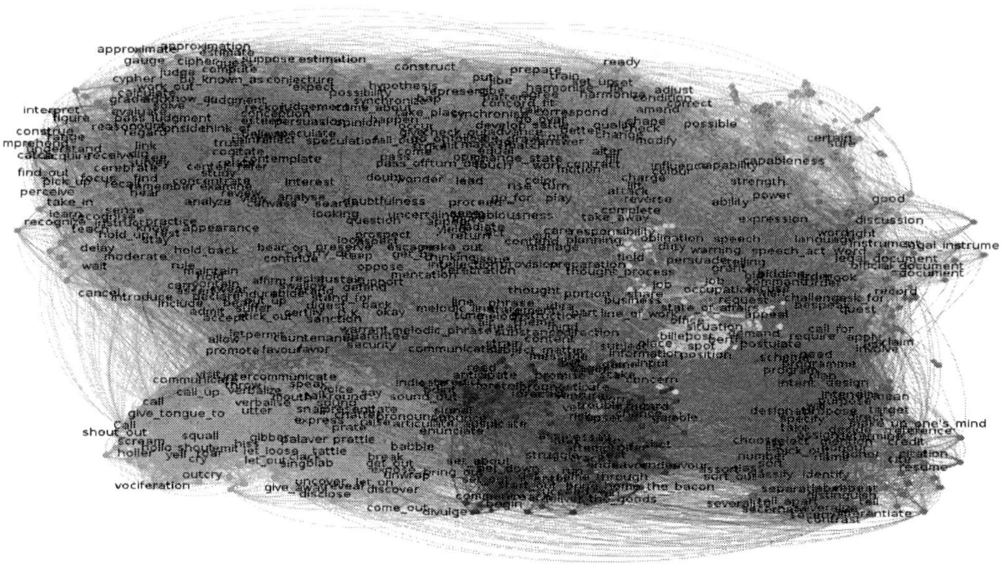

Figure 7: Generated word graph based on WordNet relations for ACE-MK cues.

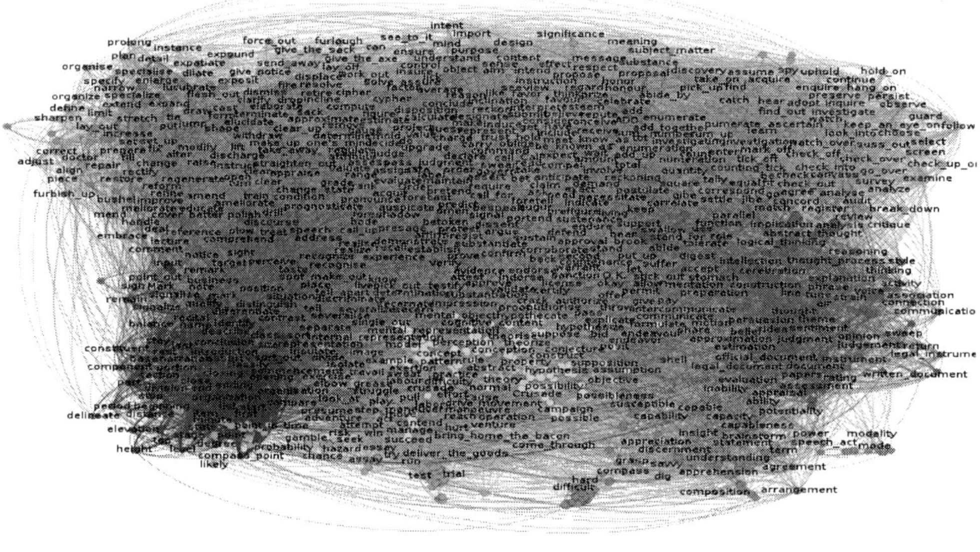

Figure 8: Generated word graph based on WordNet relations for GENIA-MK cues.

Detecting Sarcasm is Extremely Easy ;-)

Natalie Parde and **Rodney D. Nielsen**
Human Intelligence and Language Technologies (HiLT) Laboratory
Department of Computer Science and Engineering
University of North Texas
{natalie.parde, rodney.nielsen}@unt.edu

Abstract

Detecting sarcasm in text is a particularly challenging problem in computational semantics, and its solution may vary across different types of text. We analyze the performance of a domain-general sarcasm detection system on datasets from two very different domains: Twitter, and Amazon product reviews. We categorize the errors that we identify with each, and make recommendations for addressing these issues in NLP systems in the future.

1 Introduction

Sarcasm detection is a tricky problem, even for humans. The definition of sarcasm is hazy, sarcasm can be heavily context-dependent, and it is often marked more by prosodic cues than syntactic characteristics, all of which make its computational detection particularly complex. Nonetheless, some researchers have achieved success in predicting whether or not instances of text contain sarcasm based on domain-specific features (Maynard and Greenwood, 2014; Rajadesingan et al., 2015), sentiment (Riloff et al., 2013), text patterns (Davidov et al., 2010), and other semantic features (Ghosh et al., 2015; Amir et al., 2016).

Since most prior work in this area has been domain-specific, the findings resulting from these models may not be broadly applicable. For example, Twitter, a popular domain for sarcasm researchers, constrains posts to 140 (or as of very recently, 280) characters; this means that the type of sarcasm found in tweets may be quite different from that found in a domain that allows lengthy posts, such as Amazon product reviews. Previously, we explored this phenomenon by experimenting with various models to identify an approach better capable of learning domain-general sarcasm detection (Parde and Nielsen, 2017) . In this paper, we build upon that work by conducting a performance analysis of our best-performing approach on two different text domains, and identifying common types of errors made by the system. We follow this with recommendations for improvement in future sarcasm detection systems.

2 Background

Research on automatic sarcasm detection to date has taken place on a variety of domains, including news articles (Burfoot and Baldwin, 2009), web forums (Justo et al., 2014), product reviews (Buschmeier et al., 2014), and tweets (Maynard and Greenwood, 2014; Rajadesingan et al., 2015; Liebrecht et al., 2013; Riloff et al., 2013; Bamman and Smith, 2015; González-Ibáñez et al., 2011; Reyes et al., 2013; Ghosh et al., 2015; Amir et al., 2016). The last of these, Twitter-based sarcasm detection, has dominated the research arena.

Twitter is a popular domain choice for sarcasm researchers because tweets are readily-available and may be freely downloaded, and moreover many tweets are self-labeled by Twitter users for various attributes using *hashtags*, or keywords prefaced with the "#" symbol. However, tweets are not necessarily representative of text in general. Their strict length requirement causes users to adopt sometimes-confusing acronyms and shorthand spellings. Hashtags often consist of smashed-together words without any token markers, and may convey critical content not otherwise detectable in the tweet text. Finally, tweets may refer to external context that renders them confusing to later readers. For example, tweeting "Great." minutes after an election is called may be easily understandable to readers at that moment, but ambiguous to readers who see the tweet several days later, and much too vague for today's computational sarcasm detector to decipher.

Researchers who have focused on detecting sarcasm in tweets have taken several approaches.

Proceedings of the Workshop on Computational Semantics beyond Events and Roles (SemBEaR-2018), pages 21–26
New Orleans, Louisiana, June 5, 2018. ©2017 Association for Computational Linguistics

Maynard and Greenwood (2014) learned hashtags that commonly correspond with sarcastic tweets, and checked for those in subsequent tweets to determine whether or not the tweets were sarcastic. Other researchers utilized Twitter histories, developing behavioral models of sarcasm usage specific to individual users (Rajadesingan et al., 2015), or features based on the users, their audiences, and the author-audience relationship of the tweet in question (Bamman and Smith, 2015). Some researchers considered the sentiment (Riloff et al., 2013) or emotional scenario (Reyes et al., 2013) of a tweet when deciding whether or not it contained sarcasm, and finally others experimented with n-grams (Liebrecht et al., 2013) and word embeddings (Ghosh et al., 2015; Ghosh and Veale, 2016; Amir et al., 2016).

Amazon product reviews, which have also interested sarcasm researchers, differ from tweets in several key ways: they are of variable (and often much longer) length, they do not utilize hashtags, and they generally contain more context. The primary domain-specific feature employed by sarcasm detection researchers using Amazon product reviews has been a product's "star rating" (the number of stars assigned to the product by the review writer) (Buschmeier et al., 2014; Parde and Nielsen, 2017). Other characteristics that researchers have considered in this domain include syntactic features (Buschmeier et al., 2014; Davidov et al., 2010) and the presence of interjections or laughter terms (Buschmeier et al., 2014).

Finally, we learned a general sarcasm detection model from many tweets and fewer Amazon product reviews (Parde and Nielsen, 2017). We found that by applying a domain adaptation step prior to training the model, we were able to achieve higher performance in predicting sarcasm in Amazon product reviews over models that trained on reviews alone or on a simple combination of reviews and tweets. Our prior work was notable in that it was the first approach that specifically sought domain-generality. We analyze its performance on different datasets in this work.

3 Sarcasm Detection Methods

We train our sarcasm detection approach on the same training data used in our previous work (3998 tweets and 1003 Amazon product reviews), and apply it to two test datasets: AMAZON, a 251-instance set of sarcastic (87) and non-sarcastic (164) Amazon product reviews originally collected by Filatova (2012), and TWITTER, a 1000-instance set of sarcastic (391) and non-sarcastic (609) tweets containing the hashtags *#sarcasm* (the sarcastic class) or *#happiness*, *#sadness*, *#anger*, *#surprise*, *#fear*, or *#disgust* (the negative class).[1] The approach utilizes features that seek to convey informative characteristics from the domains considered as well as general characteristics expected to remain indicative of sarcasm across many domains. We briefly describe each in Table 1; for additional information, the reader is referred to our earlier paper.

3.1 Classification Algorithm

All features were extracted from each instance, regardless of its domain (feature values were left empty when it was impossible to fill them, e.g., star rating for tweets). Then, the feature space was transformed using the domain adaptation approach originally outlined by Daumé III (2007). Daumé's approach works by modifying the feature space such that it contains three mappings of the original features: a source version, a target version, and a general version. More formally, letting $\breve{\mathcal{X}} = \mathbb{R}^{3F}$ be the augmented version of a feature space $\mathcal{X} = \mathbb{R}^F$, and $\Phi^s, \Phi^t : \mathcal{X} \rightarrow \breve{\mathcal{X}}$ be mappings for the source and target data, respectively,

$$\Phi^s(\mathbf{x}) = \langle \mathbf{x}, \mathbf{0}, \mathbf{x} \rangle, \quad \Phi^t(\mathbf{x}) = \langle \mathbf{0}, \mathbf{x}, \mathbf{x} \rangle \qquad (1)$$

where $\mathbf{0} = \langle 0, 0, ..., 0 \rangle \in \mathbb{R}^F$ is the zero vector. It is then left to the classification algorithm to decide how to best take advantage of this supplemental information. We use Naïve Bayes, following our earlier work.

4 Model Performance

We compute precision (P), recall (R), and f-measure (F_1) on the positive (sarcastic) class for both TWITTER and AMAZON, and report results relative to the performance of other systems on the same data (Table 2). Our results on AMAZON are identical to those reported originally (Parde and Nielsen, 2017). Our previous paper reported results on TWITTER when training only on Twitter data; here we instead apply the same model as applied to AMAZON and achieve slightly higher results. Thus, the approach outperforms other sar-

[1]These hashtags were removed prior to using the data.

Feature Type	Description
CONTAINS TWITTER INDICATOR	Multiple binary features indicating whether the instance contains one of the sarcasm-related hashtags, emoticons, and/or indicator phrases learned by Maynard and Greenwood (2014).
TWITTER-BASED PREDICATES AND SITUATIONS	Multiple binary features indicating whether the instance contains a positive predicate, positive sentiment, and/or negative situation phrase learned by Riloff et al. (2013) from a corpus of tweets. Includes an additional binary feature that indicates whether one of those positive predicates or sentiments precedes one of those negative situation phrases by ≤ 5 tokens.
STAR RATING	The number of stars (1-5) associated with the review.
LAUGHTER AND INTERJECTIONS	Multiple binary features indicating whether the instance contains: *hahaha, haha, hehehe, hehe, jajaja, jaja, lol, lmao, rofl, wow, ugh,* and/or *huh*.
SPECIFIC CHARACTERS	Multiple binary features indicating whether the instance contains an ellipsis, an exclamation mark, and/or a question mark.
POLARITY	Multiple features indicating the most polar (positive or negative) unigram in the instance, the polarity score (-5 to +5) associated with that unigram, the average polarity of the instance, the overall (sum) polarity for the instance, the largest difference in polarity between any two words in the instance, and the percentages of positive and negative words in the instance.
SUBJECTIVITY	The percentages of strongly subjective positive words, strongly subjective negative words, weakly subjective positive words, and weakly subjective negative words in the instance.
PMI	Multiple features indicating the pointwise mutual information (PMI) between the most polar unigram and the 1, 2, 3, and 4 words that immediately follow it.
CONSECUTIVE CHARACTERS	Multiple features indicating the highest number of consecutive repeated characters in the instance (e.g., "Sooooo" $\Rightarrow$ 5) and the highest number of consecutive punctuation characters in the instance.
ALL-CAPS	Multiple features indicating the number and percentage of all-caps words in the instance.
BAG OF WORDS	Two types of bag-of-words features: one in which the words included in the "bag" are those most closely associated with four groups of training instances (Sarcastic $\times$ Non-Sarcastic) $\times$ (Amazon $\times$ Twitter), and one in which the words in the "bag" were the most common words in those groups (any duplicates across groups were removed).

Table 1: Features included in the sarcasm detection system.

		P	R	F_1
TWITTER	Parde and Nielsen (2017)	0.55	0.62	0.58
	Our Results	0.53	**0.68**	**0.59**
AMAZON	Buschmeier et al. (2014)	0.82	0.69	0.74
	Our Results	0.75	**0.82**	**0.78**

Table 2: Performance of our sarcasm detection model relative to prior work on the same datasets.

	Amazon	Twitter
Predicted Sarcastic	24	235
Predicted Non-Sarcastic	16	127

Table 3: Errors included in the analysis.

casm detection methods on both AMAZON and TWITTER.

5 Error Analysis

5.1 Methodology

We conduct our error analysis on all misclassified instances (402 total) in both AMAZON and TWITTER. The errors were distributed as shown in Table 3. For both datasets, there were more false positives (instances predicted to be sarcastic when they really weren't) than false negatives.

We analyzed each misclassified instance, making notes regarding characteristics that may have led to the misclassification. We then compiled these notes into more general error categories, identified (with examples from our data) in Tables 4 and 5. Some instances were assigned to multiple error categories.

5.2 Results

There were several leading trends in the misclassifications. Among false negatives in both datasets, in many cases the sarcasm expressed could only be inferred using world knowledge (an example tweet from this category, noted in Table 4, is *When my 10 yr old niece texts me to let me know she is taller than me. #thanks #sarcasm #hateyoubutloveyou*). Within tweets specifically, some (23) did not convey sarcasm once the sarcasm hashtag was removed. Some (8) also contained sarcastic content only in other hashtags associated with the tweet. Other tweets (13) were found upon manual inspection to not be sarcastic, despite containing the sarcasm hashtag; instead, these tweets discussed sarcasm in some way.

Nine false negatives contained words typically associated with sarcasm; developing better ways of identifying these words could eliminate such errors. For product reviews, a common trait of misclassified instances was that they developed sarcastic stories about the product (for instance, one review describes the magical qualities of a pair of

Type	Amazon	Twitter	Example
Requires World Knowledge	7	63	*When my 10 yr old niece texts me to let me know she is taller than me. #thanks #sarcasm #hateyoubutloveyou*
Formatted as Story	4	0	*I thought that I had shrunk everything in the dryer, so I gave up and put on these new Hanes cushioned crews. Immediately, I felt a sense of joy. It was strange, like the first time you kiss someone, or how you felt as a kid when waking up on Christmas morning. I kept wondering if it was the socks that made me feel that way, or if I was just somehow subconsciously triggered to reminisce. That day, in it's entirety, was wonderful. At least 50 people I had never spoken to before somehow knew my name. These were people on the street, even. At the coffee shop, the girl who normally had the demeanor of a disgruntled, middle-age cafeteria worker actually gave me a free coffee and tried to flirt with me. Not just to flirt, but a stumbly sort of flirting that only comes about when desire has made you lose your grasp of language structure. At the university, I was excused from an upcoming midterm for a reason I don't even remember. I think it involved being "an attentive enough listener at lectures."*
Positive Sentiment + Negative Situation	0	9	*#HappyBirthdayTwitter Thanks for providing a platform where people can troll and abuse each other #sarcasm*
Negative Sentiment + Positive Situation	0	3	*No one's awake at home, should've gone to the gym. Life is tough doing nothing all day #messyhouse #nodinner #sarcasm*
Highly Negative	1	3	*Don't waste your money on this convoluted and unfriendly piece of overpriced junk. ... If you find out too slowly how lousy this item is, you are stuck with it. And don't give it as a gift at Xmas - your recipients can't return it either. You have given them an expensive paperweight unless all the stars are in alignment for them, andthen they'll probably find it useless anyway.*
Many All-Caps Words	0	6	*My brain at 3am = ALWAYS A GREAT TIME. #sarcasm*
Requires #sarcasm	0	23	*Some people know how to really make you feel valued #sarcasm*
Sarcasm in Hashtags	0	8	*Oh hi LA! Long time no see! #sarcasm #yesterday #IneedALLTHENAPS*
Contains Sarcastic Word or Phrase	0	9	*Not jealous at all of anyone who could afford a pair of the #IrregularChoice #AliceInWonderland shoes today. Ohh no, not at all. #sarcasm*
Mostly Non-Sarcastic with Some Sarcastic Phrases	4	1	*I drive a Toyota Sienna minivan with JBL stuff on my speakers. Apparently that was important. Now it works great. Reception in Houston has been great. It plays through the line-in Aux port great (I use it with my ipod and creative zen) and USB keys work. I'm not sure it ever shows the file names it's playing off the USB, which is weird but not worth $100 to upgrade to a better stereo. So, it works but had quite a bit of fiddling to make it go. It's great for the $. I have fairly low standards...I only listen to audiobooks, podcasts, NPR, etc. So I have no idea what the audiophiles would think. (and, for the snarky, YES, there was a sale on the word "great" today.)*
Non-Sarcastic	1	13	*I was being sarcastic with that tweet by the way incase people thought I was serious.... #sarcasm*

Table 4: Errors: Instances incorrectly predicted as non-sarcastic.

socks at length); in such stories there tend to be particularly few linguistic indicators of sarcasm.

False positives were typified by different characteristics. Many tweets (109) in this category included excessive punctuation, a trait commonly associated with sarcastic text. Other instances (29 tweets and 5 product reviews) contained a mix of positive and negative sentiment, which the model mistook for sarcasm. Some misclassified instances contained many technical or "niche" words, for which few of the polarity-based features could have been computed, and others included ambiguous phrases often found in sarcastic text (e.g., ***Jeez**, how am I supposed to react to meeting someone who identifies her spirit animal as Claire Underwood? #HouseOfCards #Fear*). Some tweets contained misspellings that may have confused the model, and some product reviews were non-sarcastic reviews of "silly" products. In the case of these latter reviews, the model may have simply learned to mark any reviews associated with those products as sarcastic. Finally, upon manual inspection we found that four of the Amazon product reviews marked as non-sarcastic actually contained at least some sarcastic text, and 27 of the tweets that did not contain the sarcasm hashtag were in fact sarcastic.

5.3 Recommendations

Based on our analysis, we recommend that the following factors be taken into account in future systems. Beyond their anticipated direct bene-

Type	Amazon	Twitter	Example
Odd Product/Product that Seems Sarcastic	5	0	*I haven't had the chance to use it yet as the whip is broken. I'm hoping I can either get a replacement whip or just get my money back.*
Mix of Positive and Negative Sentiment	5	29	*Good morning. Coffee. Portfolio. Torment. School. #school #sadness*
Very Negative	6	5	*This book is so terrible that I couldn't even make it past the first 1/4 of it - the characters were horrible, shallow people, and the plot is so see-through. Clearly, this book is one of Sophie's earlier works - the "plot" is terrible. Don't waste your money - don't take a chance in case you crack the spine - you won't be able to return it!*
Very Positive	0	9	*Be happy. Not because everything is good, but because u can see the good side of everything #happiness*
Ambiguous Phrases	2	26	*Jeez, how am I supposed to react to meeting someone who identifies her spirit animal as Claire Underwood? #HouseOfCards #Fear*
Contains Technical Terminology	3	31	*But it's not much louder than the two-stage oillube compressor it replaced. I needed something that could be moved in a pinch, something that could run off 110V 15A service I have in the garage, and something with enough capacity to run my air ratchets, cut off tools, etc.*
Lots of Punctuation	3	109	*#SongToday WORK by @rihanna heavyyyyyyyyy!!!!! #fancy #happiness*
Short	3	11	*Oh exams coming up #sadness*
Many All-Caps Words	1	14	*Episode 42 of @TTGpodcast is outstanding! I was like "yeah good qustion Rocket–OMG THAT WAS ME I ASKED THAT!!" #surprise*
Contains Misspellings	0	13	*Thank u Spring for this beautuful snow #Spring #snow #Surprise*
Sarcastic	4	27	*I'm truly thrilled to find out which of my bodily fluids will start leaking next. Is there a bingo card for the third trimester? #surprise*

Table 5: Errors: Instances incorrectly predicted as sarcastic.

fits, adopting these recommendations should decrease reliance on syntactic features (e.g., excessive punctuation and all-caps words).

World Knowledge: For many false negatives, the sarcasm expressed was detectable only through knowledge of the world. Frame-semantic resources could be used to detect some sarcasm instantiated through script-based inconsistencies. Furthermore, features could be derived from commonsense knowledge bases such as that of the Never-Ending Language Learner (Mitchell et al., 2015) to better detect contradictory expressions.

Text Normalization: When detecting sarcasm in user-generated content (e.g., Twitter), word splitting algorithms should be applied in the future to disambiguate compound hashtags into their constituent words, and spelling correction algorithms can be applied to normalize text. The latter should be done with caution, as in some cases, spelling normalization may not be desirable—for instance, "sooooo" may convey something different from "so," while "mihgt" likely conveys the same information as "might."

Enhanced Lexicon of Sentiment and Situation Phrases: Some of the errors we identified could have been easily addressed had the system understood that they described negative situations in positive terms, or vice versa. We attempted to capture this phenomenon by employing features based on the work of Riloff et al. (2013). However, we found that the phrases identified by Riloff et al. were virtually non-existent in our Twitter dataset. To properly employ these types of features, new events and sentiment phrases should be continually mined from Twitter to account for evolving linguistic patterns and trends in public opinion.

6 Conclusion

In this work, we analyze the performance of a domain-general sarcasm detection approach on two datasets: TWITTER and AMAZON. We verify that the approach outperforms others on the same data, and conduct an analysis of the misclassified instances to identify common error types. Finally, we make recommendations for addressing these errors. It is our hope that these insights will enable researchers to build high-performing sarcasm detection systems suited to many text domains.

Acknowledgements

This material is based upon work supported by the NSF Graduate Research Fellowship Program under Grant 1144248, and the NSF under Grant 1262860. Any opinions, findings, and conclusions or recommendations expressed in this material are those of the author(s) and do not necessarily reflect the views of the National Science Foundation.

References

Silvio Amir, Byron C Wallace, Hao Lyu, Paula Carvalho, and Mario J Silva. 2016. Modelling context with user embeddings for sarcasm detection in social media. In *Proceedings of The 20th SIGNLL Conference on Computational Natural Language Learning*, pages 167–177.

David Bamman and Noah A Smith. 2015. Contextualized sarcasm detection on twitter. In *Proceedings of the Ninth International AAAI Conference on Web and Social Media*, pages 574–577.

Clint Burfoot and Timothy Baldwin. 2009. Automatic satire detection: Are you having a laugh? In *Proceedings of the ACL-IJCNLP 2009 Conference Short Papers*, pages 161–164, Suntec, Singapore. Association for Computational Linguistics.

Konstantin Buschmeier, Philipp Cimiano, and Roman Klinger. 2014. An impact analysis of features in a classification approach to irony detection in product reviews. In *Proceedings of the 5th Workshop on Computational Approaches to Subjectivity, Sentiment and Social Media Analysis*, pages 42–49, Baltimore, Maryland. Association for Computational Linguistics.

Hal Daumé III. 2007. Frustratingly easy domain adaptation. In *Proceedings of the 45th Annual Meeting of the Association of Computational Linguistics*, pages 256–263, Prague, Czech Republic. Association for Computational Linguistics.

Dmitry Davidov, Oren Tsur, and Ari Rappoport. 2010. Semi-supervised recognition of sarcasm in twitter and amazon. In *Proceedings of the Fourteenth Conference on Computational Natural Language Learning*, pages 107–116, Uppsala, Sweden. Association for Computational Linguistics.

Elena Filatova. 2012. Irony and sarcasm: Corpus generation and analysis using crowdsourcing. In *Proceedings of the Eight International Conference on Language Resources and Evaluation*, Istanbul, Turkey. European Language Resources Association.

Aniruddha Ghosh and Tony Veale. 2016. Fracking sarcasm using neural network. In *Proceedings of the 7th Workshop on Computational Approaches to Subjectivity, Sentiment and Social Media Analysis*, pages 161–169, San Diego, California. Association for Computational Linguistics.

Debanjan Ghosh, Weiwei Guo, and Smaranda Muresan. 2015. Sarcastic or not: Word embeddings to predict the literal or sarcastic meaning of words. In *Proceedings of the 2015 Conference on Empirical Methods in Natural Language Processing*, pages 1003–1012, Lisbon, Portugal. Association for Computational Linguistics.

Roberto González-Ibáñez, Smaranda Muresan, and Nina Wacholder. 2011. Identifying sarcasm in twitter: A closer look. In *Proceedings of the 49th Annual Meeting of the Association for Computational Linguistics: Human Language Technologies*, pages 581–586, Portland, Oregon, USA. Association for Computational Linguistics.

Raquel Justo, Thomas Corcoran, Stephanie M. Lukin, Marilyn Walker, and M. Ins Torres. 2014. Extracting relevant knowledge for the detection of sarcasm and nastiness in the social web. *Knowledge-Based Systems*, 69:124 – 133.

Christine Liebrecht, Florian Kunneman, and Antal Van den Bosch. 2013. The perfect solution for detecting sarcasm in tweets #not. In *Proceedings of the 4th Workshop on Computational Approaches to Subjectivity, Sentiment and Social Media Analysis*, pages 29–37, Atlanta, Georgia. Association for Computational Linguistics.

Diana Maynard and Mark Greenwood. 2014. Who cares about sarcastic tweets? investigating the impact of sarcasm on sentiment analysis. In *Proceedings of the Ninth International Conference on Language Resources and Evaluation*, Reykjavik, Iceland. European Language Resources Association.

Tom Mitchell, William Cohen, Estevam Hruschka, Partha Talukdar, Justin Betteridge, Andrew Carlson, Bhavana D. Mishra, Matthew Gardner, Bryan Kisiel, Jayant Krishnamurthy, Ni Lao, Kathryn Mazaitis, Thahir Mohamed, Ndapa Nakashole, Emmanouil A. Platanios, Alan Ritter, Mehdi Samadi, Burr Settles, Richard Wang, Derry Wijaya, Abhinav Gupta, Xinlei Chen, Abulhair Saparov, Malcolm Greaves, and Joel Welling. 2015. Never-ending learning. In *Proceedings of the Twenty-Ninth AAAI Conference on Artificial Intelligence (AAAI-15)*, pages 2302–2310.

Natalie Parde and Rodney Nielsen. 2017. #sarcasmdetection is soooo general! towards a domain-independent approach for detecting sarcasm. In *Proceedings of the 30th International Florida Artificial Intelligence Research Society Conference*, pages 276–281.

Ashwin Rajadesingan, Reza Zafarani, and Huan Liu. 2015. Sarcasm detection on twitter: A behavioral modeling approach. In *Proceedings of the Eighth ACM International Conference on Web Search and Data Mining*, pages 97–106. ACM.

Antonio Reyes, Paolo Rosso, and Tony Veale. 2013. A multidimensional approach for detecting irony in twitter. *Lang. Resour. Eval.*, 47(1):239–268.

Ellen Riloff, Ashequl Qadir, Prafulla Surve, Lalindra De Silva, Nathan Gilbert, and Ruihong Huang. 2013. Sarcasm as contrast between a positive sentiment and negative situation. In *Proceedings of the 2013 Conference on Empirical Methods in Natural Language Processing*, pages 704–714, Seattle, Washington, USA. Association for Computational Linguistics.

GKR: the Graphical Knowledge Representation for semantic parsing

Aikaterini-Lida Kalouli
University of Konstanz
aikaterini-lida.kalouli@uni-konstanz.de

Richard Crouch
A9.com
dick.crouch@gmail.com

Abstract

This paper describes the first version of an open-source semantic parser that creates graphical representations of sentences to be used for further semantic processing, e.g. for natural language inference, reasoning and semantic similarity. The Graphical Knowledge Representation which is output by the parser is inspired by the Abstract Knowledge Representation, which separates out conceptual and contextual levels of representation that deal respectively with the subject matter of a sentence and its existential commitments. Our representation is a layered graph with each sub-graph holding different kinds of information, including one sub-graph for concepts and one for contexts. Our first evaluation of the system shows an F-score of 85% in accurately representing sentences as semantic graphs.

1 Introduction

Semantic parsing to construct graphical meaning representations is an active topic at the moment (Banarescu et al., 2013; Perera et al., 2018; Flanigan et al., 2014; Wang et al., 2015; Berant et al., 2013). It is not without its critics, however. Bender et al. (2015) object to the conflation of sentence meaning with speaker meaning, inherent in trying to use annotations to learn a direct mapping from sentences onto highly domain specific meaning representations. Bos (2016) and Stabler (2017) have also questioned the expressive power of Abstract Meaning Representation (AMR) (Banarescu et al., 2013), one of the most popular graphical meaning representations.

We believe that both lines of criticism are well-founded, but that there is still value in parsing to produce graphical representations. This paper describes the first version of an open source semantic parser that creates graphical representations that are inspired by those produced by the proprietary system described in Boston et al. (forthcoming). Salient features of the system are:

- It uses the enhanced dependencies (Schuster and Manning, 2016) of the Stanford Neural Universal Dependency parser (Chen and Manning, 2014) to create dependency graphs, on top of which fuller semantic graphs are constructed.
- Interaction between different sub-graphs is used to account for phenomena like Booleans (negation, disjunction), modals and *irrealis* contexts, distributivity and quantifier scope, co-reference, and sense selection.
- Though oriented to using formal ontologies to support a Natural Logic (MacCartney and Manning, 2007) style of Natural Language Inference (NLI), it also supports the somewhat different task of measuring semantic similarity.
- More philosophically, we view our graphs as first-class semantic objects that should be directly manipulated in reasoning and other forms of semantic processing. We do not see them as just a prettier way of writing down formulas in first- or higher-order logic.

In the next section we briefly describe the precursors and motivations behind our approach. In section 3 we present the Graphical Knowledge Representation (GKR) and how it is constructed. Section 4 evaluates the current parsing into GKR, while section 5 discusses our future additions to the system. In section 6 we compare GKR to other similar representations and parsers. In the last section we offer our conclusions and point to a companion paper discussing named graphs.

2 AKR and Layered Graphs

The so-called Abstract Knowledge Representation (AKR)[1] (Bobrow et al., 2007b,a) focused on in-

[1]AKR is the semantic component of the XLE platform (Maxwell and Kaplan, 1996)

Proceedings of the Workshop on Computational Semantics beyond Events and Roles (SemBEaR-2018), pages 27–37
New Orleans, Louisiana, June 5, 2018. ©2017 Association for Computational Linguistics

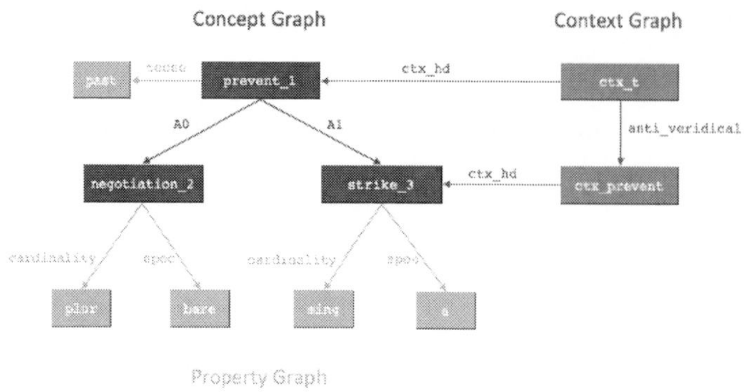

Figure 1: Concept graph (blue), property graph (yellow) and context graph (grey) from Boston et al. (forthcoming) for *Negotiations prevented a strike.*

tensional phenomena in natural language, with the sentence *Negotiations prevented a strike* being a driving example (Condoravdi et al., 2002). The claim was that, viewed in the right way, the logical formula

$$\exists n, s.\, \texttt{negotiation}(n) \wedge \texttt{strike}(s) \wedge \texttt{prevent}(n, s)$$

was a correct but incomplete semantic representation. It is correct if the variables n and s are construed as referring to sub-concepts of the concepts *negotiation* and *strike*, rather than to an individual strike or negotiation. The formula just describes the subject matter: some kind of prevention, restricted to a relation between some kind of negotiation and some kind of strike. The formula, construed as talking about concepts, makes no assertions about the existence or otherwise of any such negotiations or strikes. To complete the representation it is necessary to add a contextual level that makes assertions about whether instances of the concepts exist. In this case there are two contexts. A top level context in which the negotiation concept is asserted to have an instance; and a hypothetical (prevented) context in which the strike is claimed to have an instance. The two contexts are in an anti-veridical relationship, meaning that the *strike* concept that has an instance in the lower hypothetical context has no instance in the top context. Later work (Nairn et al., 2006) used this framework to capture a wide variety of relative polarity inferences arising from factive and implicative verbs.

A semantics for a variant of AKR was presented in the form of a Textual Inference Logic (TIL) (de Paiva et al., 2007). This recast AKR as a contexted description logic, but was not strictly faithful to AKR's eschewal of reference to individuals in favor of reference to concepts. The underlying semantics for TIL followed that of description logic by not taking concepts as primitive, but instead defining concept relations in terms of relations between sets of individuals in concept extensions.

The approach was revisited in an explicitly graphical form (Boston et al., forthcoming), recasting AKR as a set of layered sub-graphs, including a conceptual graph, a contextual graph, along with a property graph, syntactic dependency graph, a co-reference graph, and with the possibility of layering in further sub-graphs should an application demand it. The graphical representation of *Negotiations prevented a strike* is shown in Figure 1.

The graphical format was more than just notational sugar to provide more colorful and accessible representations. First, dominance in the concept and property graphs is strictly aligned with concept restriction: the parent concept is subsectively restricted by the child concept or property. Second, a strict separation between the concept and context graph is enforced: concepts cannot be restricted by contexts. Just one kind of link between contexts and concepts is permitted: a context-head that indicates the main concept that is held to have an instance within the context, but whose instantiation may flip in a higher context.

3 The Graphical Knowledge Representation

Following these motivations we implement a semantic parser that rewrites a given sentence to a layered semantic graph. The implementation of the parser is done in Java. The semantic graph consists of at least four sub-graphs, layered on top of a central conceptual (or predicate-argument) sub-graph. Each such graph encodes different information. As will be shown, this approach increases the depth of expressivity and precision because we can, if needed, ignore some sub-graphs and lose precision but we will not lose accuracy. Each semantic graph is a rooted, node-labeled, edge-labeled and directed graph that consists of a dependencies sub-graph, a conceptual sub-graph, a contextual sub-graph, a properties sub-graph and a lexical sub-graph. It can include further sub-graphs as well, such as the co-reference and the temporal sub-graphs. In the following we describe the five obligatory sub-graphs of the sentence *The boy faked the illness.* and what rewritings are required to obtain those graphs.

3.1 The Dependency Graph

The dependency graph represents the full parse of the sentence as this is produced by the Universal Dependencies (UDs). For GKR we use the Stanford CoreNLP Software to produce the dependencies and precisely to produce the enhanced++ UDs (Schuster and Manning, 2016). The enhanced++ UDs make implicit relations between content words more explicit by adding certain relations, e.g. in the case of subjects of control verbs the relation between the subject of the main verb and the control verb is marked by adding an extra edge pointing from the control verb to the subject. The enhanced++ UDs offer a very good basis for our approach because they already deal with many of the phenomena that any semantic parser needs to deal with. The output graph of the Stanford parser is rewritten to our own implementation of the dependency graph (see Figure 2) so that it conforms to the constraints of our layered semantic graph.

3.2 The Conceptual Graph

The conceptual graph shown in Figure 3 (left) contains the basic predicate-argument structure of the sentence as we can extract it from the UDs: *fake* has *boy* as one of its arguments (this is the agent,

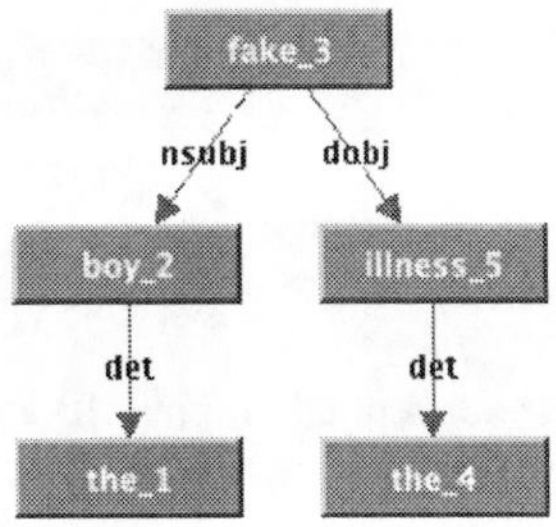

Figure 2: The dependency graph of *The boy faked the illness.*

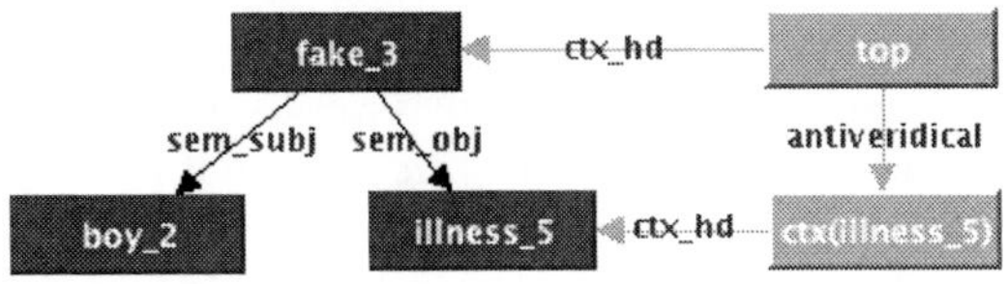

Figure 3: The conceptual graph (left) and the contextual graph (right) of *The boy faked the illness.*

the A0, the semantic-subject or whatever else any other theory might call it) and *illness* as its other argument (again, this is the patient, A1, semantic-object). The conceptual graph is the core of the semantic graph and glues all other sub-graphs together. Thus, if we just look at the concept graph, we know the subject matter of the sentence. A more formal representation might look like this: *fake(f) & boy(b) & illness(i) & agent(f,b) & patient(f,i)*. As with AKR (section 2), the variables *f*, *b*, and *i* are not individuals but concepts. The formula *illness(i)* does not say that *i* is an instance of *illness*, but that *i* is some sub-concept of the lexical concept *illness*. This means that the conceptual graph does not convey all information conveyed by the sentence; it makes no claims about the existence or otherwise of boys or illnesses. But insofar as it goes, the conceptual graph is accurate; what it expresses is correct but incomplete. It allows judgments to be made about semantic similarity between sentences, but not on its own judgments about truth or entailment. The separation of completeness from correctness, and similarity from entailment, is hard to achieve for more conventional logical representations that quantify over individuals.

3.3 The Contextual Graph

The contextual graph provides the existential commitments of the sentence. It introduces a top con-

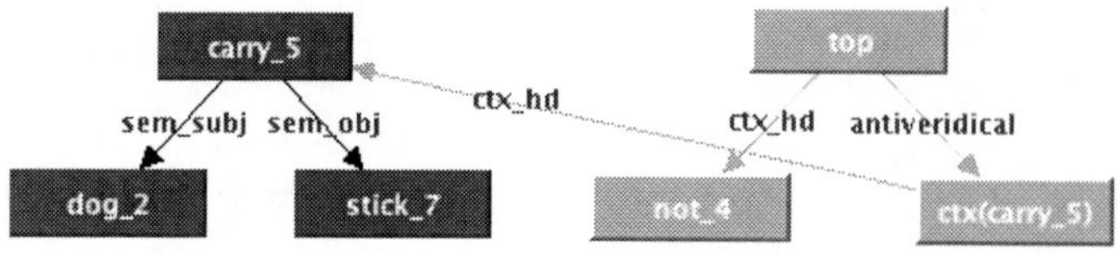

Figure 4: The conceptual graph (left) and the contextual graph (right) of *The dog is not carrying the stick.*

text (or possible world) which represents whatever the author of the sentence takes the described world to be like; in other words, whatever he/she commits to be the "true" world. Below the top context additional contexts are introduced, corresponding to any alternative worlds introduced in the sentence. Each of these embedded contexts makes commitments about its own state of affairs, principally by claiming, through the `ctx_hd` link, that the context's head concept is instantiated within that context.

Linguistic phenomena that introduce alternative worlds and thus such embedded contexts are negation, disjunction, modals, clausal contexts of belief and knowledge, implicatives and factives, imperatives, questions, conditionals, and distributivity. Apart from the latter four, the rest of the phenomena have already been implemented for this first version of the system by rewriting them to the corresponding contexts. The implicatives and factives are the only contexts that cannot be recognized and dealt with from the surface form of the sentence because their factuality predictions are inherent in their meaning. Therefore, their signatures have to be looked up. For this purpose we use the open source, extended lexicon of Stanovsky et al. (2017) which is based on the works of Karttunen (1971), Karttunen (2012) and Lotan et al. (2013). The lexicon holds more than 2,400 unique words, each assigned to a signature for positive and negative contexts. Predicates are assigned to signatures based on their finite and infinite complements. The extracted signatures are utilized for introducing the necessary contexts.

Our example sentence *The boy faked the illness.* contains such an implicative context. In its contextual graph in Figure 3 (right), the top context says that there is an instance of *faking* in which an instance of a *boy* is faking an instance of an *illness*. The top context has an edge linking it to its head *fake*, which shows that there is an instance of *faking* in this top context. The top context has a second, anti-veridical edge linking it to the context *ctx(illness)* which has *illness* as its head. This head edge asserts that there is an instance of illness in this contrary-to-fact context *ctx(illness)*. But since *ctx(illness)* and top are linked with an anti-veridical edge, it means that there is no instance of *illness* in the top world which is accurate as the illness was faked.[2] Any other concepts, e.g. *boy*, involved in the sentence but not explicitly represented in the contexts graph are taken to exist in the top context.

The introduction of contexts or possible worlds to deal with intensional predicates is familiar, though maybe not so much so when combined with reference to concepts rather than individuals. The treatment of Boolean operations like negation and disjunction through contexts is less familiar (though a feature too of AKR). Negation introduces an anti-veridical context. For the sentence *The dog is not carrying the stick.* (see Figure 4) the negated context has as its head the concept of *carrying*, restricted to be a carrying of a stick by the dog. In the negated context, it is asserted that there is an instance of this kind of *carrying*; but in the top context this concept is asserted to be uninstantiated. The impact of the negation is only seen in the context graph; the concept graph is identical for the negated and un-negated sentence. At the moment, we do not deal with morphological negation, e.g. *The boy is unhappy.*, i.e. no additional context is introduced for such negations. Such negations are dealt as normal lexical items for the moment; the mapping to the lexical resources is to account for the correct negative meaning.

Disjunction and conjunction do have an impact on the concept graph. Both introduce an additional complex concept that is the combination of the individual disjoined/conjoined concepts. Each component concept is marked in the concept graph as being an element of the complex concept (Fig-

[2]Note that definiteness does not project up through presuppositions in a way that predicts existence. Definiteness indicates that some specific kind of illness is presupposed, e.g. a (claimed) sore throat that kept the boy away from school, but not some specific individual.

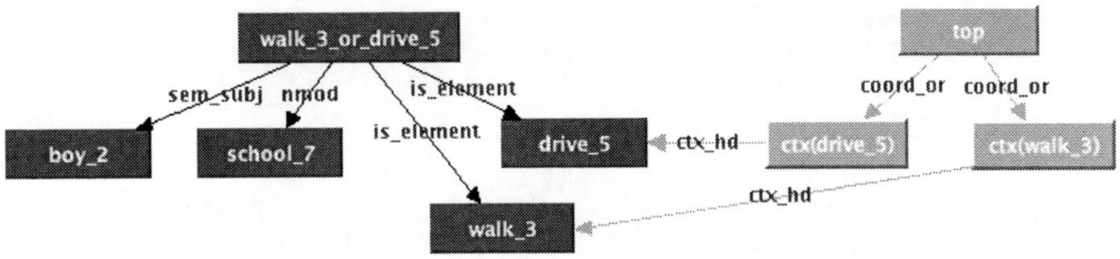

Figure 5: The conceptual graph (left) and the contextual graph (right) of *The boy walked or drove to school.*

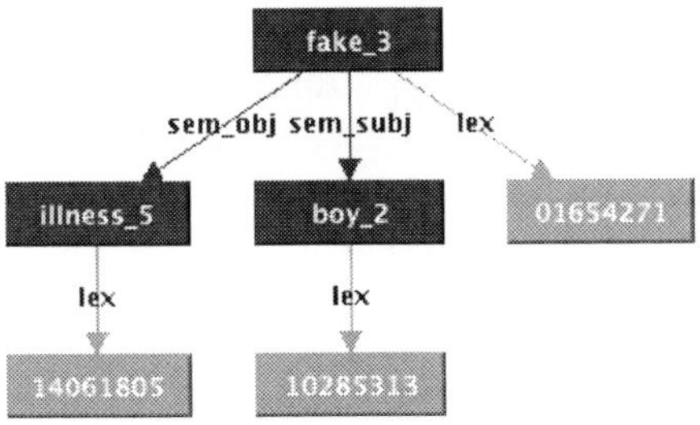

Figure 6: The lexical graph (on top of the conceptual graph) of *The boy faked the illness.*

ure 5, left). The difference between conjunction and disjunction is that disjunction introduces additional contexts for the components of the complex concept (Figure 5, right). These contexts say that in one arm of the disjunct the *walking* concept is instantiated, while in the other arm it is the *driving* concept that is instantiated. The conjunction would just say that both concepts are instantiated in the upper context.

3.4 The Properties Graph

The properties graph (Figure 7) imposes further, mostly non-lexical, restrictions on the graph. It associates the conceptual graph with morphological and syntactical features such as the cardinality of nouns, verbal tense and aspect, finiteness of specifiers, etc. For now, for building the property graph we use our own shallow morphological analysis that is based on the Part-Of-Speech (POS) tags provided by the parser. It is clear that such an analysis cannot capture all complex nuances of phenomena like that of tense and aspect and that it only offers a simplification of those. Still, the properties graph remains accurate; it does not convey all that is there but whatever is conveyed is correct. We plan to implement a temporal graph which is expected to account for the current simplification.

3.5 The Lexical Graph

The lexical graph of Figure 6 carries the lexical information of the sentence. It associates each node of the conceptual graph with its disambiguated sense and concept, its hypernyms and its hyponyms, making use of JIGSAW[3] by Basile et al. (2007), WordNet[4] by Fellbaum (1998) and SUMO[5] by Niles and Pease (2001) and Pease (2011). For building the lexical graph, the whole sentence is first run through the knowledge-based JIGSAW algorithm which disambiguates each word of the sentence by assigning it the sense with the highest probability. Briefly, JIGSAW exploits the WordNet senses and uses a different disambiguation strategy for each part of speech, taking into account the context of each word. It scores each WordNet sense of the word based on its probability to be correct in that context. The sense with the highest score is chosen as the disambiguated sense and is added as a new node to the lexical graph, with an edge linking the word to its sense. Although the sense is the only lexical information that is visible on the graph, there is more information encoded behind this sense node. Firstly, we encode the SUMO concept corresponding to the disambiguated sense. SUMO is the largest, publicly available ontology that maps WordNet senses to concepts (Niles and Pease, 2003). We access our local copy of the SUMO ontology and extract the concept mapped to the disambiguated sense as well as the hypernyms and hyponyms corresponding to that sense and concept. This information is then stored within the node so that it is easily accessible at all times. The lexical graph can and will be expanded with more information like the one coming from word embeddings. We plan to integrate this component at the next stage of our work.

[3]Available under https://github.com/pippokill/JIGSAW
[4]Available under http://wordnet.princeton.edu/
[5]Available under http://www.ontologyportal.org

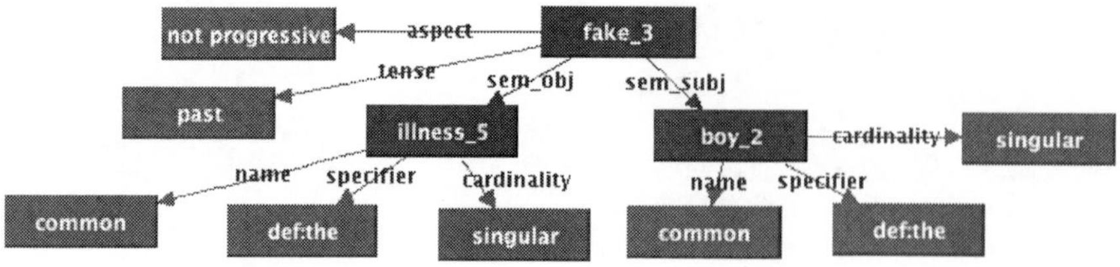

Figure 7: The property graph (on top of the conceptual graph) of *The boy faked the illness.*

4 Evaluation of GKR

4.1 Intrinsic Evaluation

We would like to evaluate our semantic parser to see how many phenomena can already be accurately represented and what should still be improved or implemented. To this end, we use the HP test suite by Flickinger et al. (1987), an extensive test suite with various kinds of syntactic and semantic phenomena, originally created for the evaluation of parsers and other NLP systems. The test suite features 1250 sentences dealing with some 290 distinct syntactic and semantic phenomena and sub-phenomena. Some of the contained sentences are ungrammatical on purpose (and marked as such). For our testing we chose to use a subset of the test suite consisting of 781 sentences (and 180 phenomena, an average of 4.3 sentences pro phenomenon). We decided to exclude ungrammatical sentences (314) and sentences with typos (20) since our testing is aiming at testing the coverage of the semantic graphs and not the accuracy of the parser — which we inevitably and indirectly do as will be shown shortly. We also excluded all sentences (135) with conditionals, anaphora and ellipsis phenomena because such cases are still under implementation and thus yet not part of our system. The test set does not include challenging lexical semantics phenomena, e.g. polysemous words, as it aims at the coverage of syntactic and deeper semantic phenomena. We run the test set of 781 sentences through our semantic parser and got human-readable representations of the semantic graphs which 2 annotators manually evaluated for their correctness. A representation was judged *correct* when the concepts, contexts and properties sub-graphs exactly capture the information they should. If the dependency graph is wrong, then the whole representation is labelled as *parser_error*. Erroneous syntactic parsing will always produce erroneous conceptual and contextual graphs, which we do not deal with at the moment. The lexical sub-graph was also not judged for the correctness of the selected senses as this would result in evaluating the disambiguation algorithm and the coverage of the lexical resources themselves, which is not the goal of this work. However, any failures in the lexical resources and thus in the lexical sub-graph do not have an impact on the rest of the graphs, which again confirms the flexibility of the layered graph approach. The results of the manual evaluation are shown in Table 1.

Label	Sentences	Percentage
correct	591	75.6%
false	5	0.6%
parser_error	185	23.6%
Total	**781**	

Table 1: Evaluation results.

Table 1 shows that 185 cases could not be correctly parsed by the Stanford Parser and thus the output semantic representation is inevitably wrong as well. From the remaining 596 sentences for which a correct parse was given, 591 were rewritten to correct semantic graphs and 5 had semantic graphs with missing or wrong information. The overall performance of the system can be seen in Table 2. The initial version of our semantic parser achieves an F-score of 85% when tested on this subset of the HP test suite. Although this test suite and evaluation are not exhaustive, the performance of the system delivers promising results. Note that the relative quality of the integrated tools, e.g. the syntactic parser, the implicatives-factives lexicon,

Metric	Percentage
Precision	0.99
Recall	0.76
F-score	**0.85**

Table 2: Overall performance of the system.

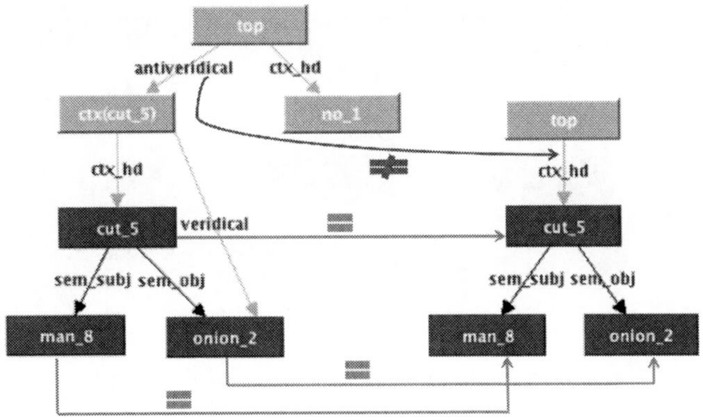

Figure 8: Schematic NLI computation for the pair *A= No onion is being cut by a man. (left) B= An onion is being cut by a man. (right).*

etc., has a direct impact on the overall quality of the semantic representations and the performance of our parser.

4.2 Schematic Computation of Natural Language Inference

We would like to very briefly demonstrate how GKR facilitates semantic processing tasks, such as natural language inference (NLI) and semantic similarity, by describing the inference computation of the pair *A = No onion is being cut by a man. B= An onion is being cut by a man.*[6] For doing NLI (see Figure 8) we determine specificity relations[7] between pairs of individual concept nodes, one from the premise (A) and one more from the hypothesis (B) sentence. In the figure these correspond to equality relations and are represented by the orange arrows. These initial specificity judgments can then be updated with any further restrictions placed on the nodes from the properties and lexical graphs. The context graph is then used to determine which concepts are instantiated or uninstantiated within which contexts. In our example, we can see that *cut* is instantiated, i.e. is the *ctx_head* of the top of B but is antiveridical in the top of A. Similarly, in B *onion* is veridical in top (and therefore it is not explicitly represented) while in A it is veridical only in context of *cut* and since *ctx(cut)* is antiveridical in top, *onion* is also antiveridical in top through transitivity. As a final step for inference, instantiation and specificity are combined to determine entailment relations.

In the same process, if we choose to ignore the context graphs and the instantiation of concepts, we can also measure semantic similarity — which does not require judgments about truth or entailment. The semantic similarity between the two sentences can be measured on the basis of the concepts graphs of the sentences. Since the concept graph represents "what is talked about", the comparison of the concepts graphs can compute the overall similarity by computing the similarity of the different concept pairs of the two sentences and merging them together.

5 Future Work

At this point, old-school semanticists will probably be asking: but what about quantifier scope? This is a rarer phenomenon than the literature would have you believe. The primary reading for a sentence like *Three boys ate five pizzas* involves no scope variation: there were just three boys and five pizzas, and eating. This cumulative reading is difficult to express in standard logical representations without recourse to branching quantifiers, or to treating three and five not as generalized quantifiers but as cardinality restrictions on existential quantifiers. It is an inelegance that scoped readings are the default in these representations, while being the exception in practice.

That being said, quantifier scope — or rather, distributivity — does occur; *take two tablets three times* really does involve six tablets. We regard distributivity as context inducing (Figure 9). The distributional context has two arcs into the concept graph. In addition to the normal context head arc,

[6]The pair comes from the SICK corpus (Marelli et al., 2014).

[7]The specificity relations are taken as discussed in MacCartney and Manning (2007) and Crouch and King (2007).

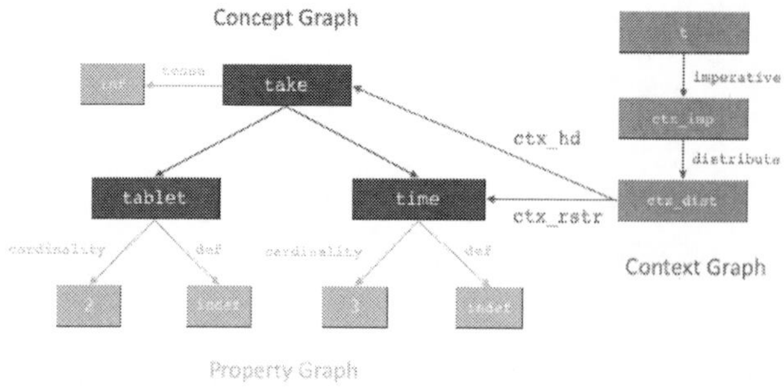

Figure 9: Distributivity for *Take two tablets three times.*

which marks the body of the distribution, there is a context restriction arc that marks the concept to be distributed over: in this case the *times* that comprise individual sub-concepts of the concept *3-times*; see (van den Berg et al., 2001) for more details on individual sub-concepts. For each individual sub-concept in the distributive restriction, there is asserted to be an instance of the head concept further restricted by the individual sub-concept.

Distributive contexts are similar to our proposed conditional contexts, which also have head (consequent) and restriction (antecedent) arcs. This is reminiscent of the use of conditionals to express universal quantification in Discourse Representation Theory (Kamp and Reyle, 1993). That quantification is treated as having a modal aspect should not be that surprising. In first order modal logic, modal operators switch the context of evaluation of sub-formulas by altering the assignment of a possible world. Quantifiers switch the context of evaluation by altering the assignment to a variable. Both, in other words, switch contexts of evaluation. Our contextual treatment of distributivity just makes this similarity more apparent.

The proposed layered semantic graph can involve further sub-graphs as mentioned before. One of them may be the co-reference sub-graph which should link together any elements referring to the same entities, e.g. to resolve any pronouns involved or to identify two elements as "identical", i.e. as referring to the same entity. A simple example of those kinds of linking can be see in Figure 10 for the sentence *John, our neighbor, loves his wife.* Here, the pronoun *his* is resolved to its referent *John* and *John* is set as "identical" to *neighbor*. Similar co-reference graphs expanding over the level of a single sentence should be able to account for some inter-sentential semantics where the co-referring entities of different sentences, e.g.

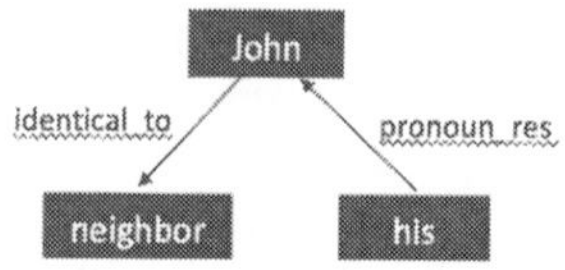

Figure 10: Co-reference graph for *John, our neighbor, loves his wife.*

of the premise and of the hypothesis in the natural language inference task, are inter-connected to each other and thus facilitate the further processing.

6 Related Work

How does GKR differ from its precursor, AKR? While the two representations are very close, they differ in that a) AKR is based on the syntax produced by LFG while GKR is based on UDs and that b) AKR is rather flat-structured while GKR is based on graphs. Although LFG is probably more informative and could offer us for free some of the features that we need to implement extra for UDs, its parsing is either not robust enough or not openly available in comparison to state-of-the-art dependency parsers. Also, it is not straightforwardly combinable with other state-of-the-art techniques that we wish to utilize, e.g. with word embeddings. Additionally, a graph-based representation is beneficial for our purposes, as already discussed in Section 1. Last but not least, AKR and its most recent revision in Boston et al. (forthcoming) is proprietary software and our intention is to produce a semantic parser that can be offered freely and openly to the community.

A more recent meaning representation is the AMR (Banarescu et al., 2013), which aims at introducing a semantic representation language with which a given sentence can be translated to its semantic formula. The representation is based on manual annotation of the structures and is thus expensive, while the attempts for automatic creation of AMRs are currently showing low accuracy (Flanigan et al., 2014; Wang et al., 2015). But this is not the only drawback: AMR ignores function words, tense, articles and prepositions which means that important information for the semantic processing remains unused. Additionally, AMR has limited expressive power for universal quantification (Bos, 2016), models negation in an inconvenient way (Bos, 2016) and does not make a distinction between real and *irrealis* events (as in our example *The boy faked the illness.*). Another disadvantage is the fact that AMR is biased towards English as pointed out by the creators. Although our system is also built for English and the lexical resources necessary are also language-dependent, the approach and GKR itself are highly language-independent. Furthermore, the fact that the sentential representation is conflated in only one graph does not facilitate semantic tasks that require stepwise access to different kinds of information, e.g. semantic similarity tasks.

A more venerable representation is DRT (Kamp and Reyle, 1993). This follows a first-order, individual based approach to predicate-argument structure rather than the concept based approach of AKR. However, the ability to name sub-Discourse Representation Structures (DRSs), and have those sub-DRSs act as arguments of (modal) predicates is very closely connected to our use of contexts. DRT shows a willingness to freely mix individual and context-denoting discourse referents, which tends to bring a highly realist approach to possible worlds in its wake. GKR, on the other hand, is careful to impose a kind of blood-brain barrier between concepts and contexts.

DepLambda (Reddy et al., 2016) uses a lambda calculus based method to transform dependencies into logical forms. Similar to GKR in availing itself of general dependency parsers, the semantic representation is essentially non-graphical, and we are unsure about how existential commitments are dealt with and whether this approach could really be practically used for the tasks of inference and reasoning. We are also skeptical about the fact that the semantic representations of semantically-identical sentences, e.g. a passive/active sentence, do not look alike, as the authors themselves observe.

Although AKR, AMR, DRT and DepLambda are the closest to our representations, there are a couple of other approaches that can be viewed as a step towards producing semantic representations for semantic processing. Firstly, there is the work of Schuster and Manning (2016) who bring UDs a step further by enhancing them with more explicit relations which are needed for any kind of further semantic processing. Their work is the basis of GKR, not only because the produced UDs are of high quality (Schuster and Manning, 2016), but also because different linguistic phenomena that can change how a semantic representation looks like are already solved, e.g. the subject of raising verbs is made explicit. There are still cases that are not optimally solved, e.g. copulas and expletives, and we hope that they can be improved in the future. A similar attempt is the system PropS by (Stanovsky et al., 2016) which is designed to explicitly express the proposition structure of a sentence. The system abstracts away from the syntactic structure by adding relations such as *outcome* and *condition* for conditionals while not becoming too abstract as AMR is. It is thus going this "next" step towards semantics without however offering a more complete semantic structure.

7 Conclusions

We have presented an expressive, graph-based semantic formalism that supports semantic parsing, as well as modal and hypothetical textual inference. Future work will account for the formal definitions of the notions presented in this paper. The first version of the parser is publicly available under `https://github.com/kkalouli/GKR_semantic_parser`. A companion paper (Crouch and Kalouli, 2018) discusses in more detail the benefits of such layered graphs for semantic representation.

References

Laura Banarescu, Claire Bonial, Shu Cai, Madalina Georgescu, Kira Griffitt, Ulf Hermjakob, Kevin Knight, Philipp Koehn, Martha Palmer, and Nathan Schneider. 2013. Abstract Meaning Representation for Sembanking. In *Proceedings of the Linguistic Annotation Workshop*.

Pierpaolo Basile, Marco de Gemmis, Anna-Lisa Gentile, Pasquale Lops, and Giovanni Semeraro. 2007. Uniba: Jigsaw algorithm for Word Sense Disambiguation. In *Proceedings of the Fourth International Workshop on Semantic Evaluations*

(SemEval-2007), pages 398–401, Prague, Czech Republic. Association for Computational Linguistics.

Emily M. Bender, Dan Flickinger, Stephan Oepen, Woodley Packard, and Ann Copestake. 2015. Layers of Interpretation: On Grammar and Compositionality. In *Proceedings of the 11th International Conference on Computational Semantics*, pages 239–249, London, UK. Association for Computational Linguistics.

J. Berant, A. Chou, R. Frostig, and P. Liang. 2013. Semantic Parsing on Freebase from Question-Answer Pairs. In *Empirical Methods in Natural Language Processing (EMNLP)*.

Martin van den Berg, Cleo Condoravdi, and Richard Crouch. 2001. Counting concepts. In *Proceedings of the Thirteenth Amsterdam Colloquium*, pages 67–72.

Danny G. Bobrow, Bob Cheslow, Cleo Condoravdi, Lauri Karttunen, Tracy Holloway-King, Rowan Nairn, Valeria de Paiva, Charlotte Price, and Annie Zaenen. 2007a. PARC's Bridge question answering system. In *Proceedings of the GEAF (Grammar Engineering Across Frameworks) 2007 Workshop*.

Danny G. Bobrow, Cleo Condoravdi, Richard Crouch, Valeria de Paiva, Lauri Karttunen, Tracy Holloway-King, Rowan Nairn, Charlotte Price, and Annie Zaenen. 2007b. Precision-focused Textual Inference. In *Proceedings of the ACL-PASCAL Workshop on Textual Entailment and Paraphrasing*, RTE '07, pages 16–21, Stroudsburg, PA, USA. Association for Computational Linguistics.

Johan Bos. 2016. Expressive Power of Abstract Meaning Representations. *Computational Linguistics*, 42(3):527–535.

Marisa Boston, Richard Crouch, Erdem Özcan, and Peter Stubley. forthcoming. Natural language inference using an ontology. In Cleo Condoravdi, editor, *Lauri Karttunen Festschrift*.

Danqi Chen and Christopher D. Manning. 2014. A Fast and Accurate Dependency Parser using Neural Networks. In *Proceedings of EMNLP 2014*.

Cleo Condoravdi, Richard Crouch, John Everett, Valeria De Paiva, Reinhard Stolle, Danny Bobrow, and Martin Van Den Berg. 2002. Preventing Existence.

Richard Crouch and Aikaterini-Lida Kalouli. 2018. Named Graphs for Semantic Representations. In *Proceedings of *SEM 2018, to appear*.

Richard Crouch and Tracy Holloway King. 2007. *Systems and methods for detecting entailment and contradiction*. US Patent 7,313,515.

C. Fellbaum. 1998. *WordNet: An Electronic Lexical Database (Language, Speech, and Communication)*. The MIT Press.

Jeffrey Flanigan, Sam Thomson, Jaime Carbonell, Chris Dyer, and Noah A. Smith. 2014. A discriminative graph-based parser for the abstract meaning representation. In *Proceedings of ACL*.

D. Flickinger, J. Nerbonne, I.A. Sag, and T. Wasow. 1987. Toward Evaluation of NLP Systems. Hewlett-Packard Laboratories. In *24th Annual Meeting of the Association for Computational Linguistics (ACL)*.

Hans Kamp and Uwe Reyle. 1993. *From Discourse to Logic. Introduction to Modeltheoretic Semantics of Natural Language, Formal Logic and Discourse Representation Theory*. Kluwer, Dordrecht.

Lauri Karttunen. 1971. Implicative verbs. *Language*, 47:340–358.

Lauri Karttunen. 2012. Simple and phrasal implicatives. In *Proceedings of *SEM 2012*, pages 124–131.

Amnon Lotan, Asher Stern, and Ido Dagan. 2013. Truthteller: Annotating Predicate Truth. In *Proceedings of NAACL-HLT 2013*, page 752–757.

Bill MacCartney and Christopher D. Manning. 2007. Natural logic for textual inference. In *Proceedings of the ACL Workshop on Textual Entailment and Paraphrasing*.

Marco Marelli, Stefano Menini, Marco Baroni, Luisa Bentivogli, Raffaella Bernardi, and Roberto Zamparelli. 2014. A SICK cure for the evaluation of compositional distributional semantic models. In *Proceedings of LREC 2014*.

John Maxwell and Ron Kaplan. 1996. An Efficient Parser for LFG. In *Proceedings of the First LFG Conference*.

Rowan Nairn, Cleo Condoravdi, and Lauri Karttunen. 2006. Computing relative polarity for textual inference. *Inference in Computational Semantics (ICoS-5)*, pages 20–41.

Ian Niles and Adam Pease. 2001. Toward a Standard Upper Ontology. In *Proceedings of the 2nd International Conference on Formal Ontology in Information Systems (FOIS-2001)*, pages 2–9.

Ian Niles and Adam Pease. 2003. Linking Lexicons and Ontologies: Mapping Wordnet to the Suggested Upper Merged Ontology. In *Proceedings of the IEEE International Conference on Information and Knowledge Engineering*, pages 412–416.

Valeria de Paiva, Danny G. Bobrow, Cleo Condoravdi, Richard Crouch, Ron Kaplan, Lauri Karttunen, Tracy Holloway-King, Rowan Nairn, and Annie Zaenen. 2007. Textual inference logic: Take two. In *Proceedings of the Workshop on Contexts and Ontologies: Representation and Reasoning, Workshop associated with the 6th International Conference on Modeling and Using Context*.

Adam Pease. 2011. *Ontology: A Practical Guide*. Articulate Software Press, Angwin, CA.

Vittorio Perera, Tagyoung Chung, Thomas Kollar, and Emma Strubell. 2018. Multi-Task Learning for parsing the Alexa Meaning Representation Language. In *Proc AAAI*.

Siva Reddy, Oscar Täckström, Michael Collins, Tom Kwiatkowski, Dipanjan Das, Mark Steedman, and Mirella Lapata. 2016. Transforming Dependency Structures to Logical Forms for Semantic Parsing. *Transactions of the Association for Computational Linguistics*, 4:127–140.

Sebastian Schuster and Christopher D. Manning. 2016. Enhanced English Universal Dependencies: An Improved Representation for Natural Language Understanding Tasks. In *Proceedings of the Tenth International Conference on Language Resources and Evaluation (LREC 2016)*.

Ed Stabler. 2017. Reforming AMR. In *Formal Grammar 2017. Lecture Notes in Computer Science*, volume 10686. Springer.

Gabriel Stanovsky, Judith Eckle-Kohler, Yevgeniy Puzikov, Ido Dagan, and Iryna Gurevych. 2017. Integrating Deep Linguistic Features in Factuality Prediction over Unified Datasets. In *Proceedings of the 55th Annual Meeting of the Association for Computational Linguistics (Short Papers)*, pages 352–357.

Gabriel Stanovsky, Jessica Ficler, Ido Dagan, and Yoan Goldberg. 2016. Getting More Out Of Syntax with Props. *CoRR*, abs/1603.01648.

Chuan Wang, Nianwen Xue, and Sameer Pradhan. 2015. A transition-based algorithm for AMR parsing. In *Proceedings of the 2015 Conference of the North American Chapter of the Association for Computational Linguistics: Human Language Technologies*.

Computational Argumentation: A Journey Beyond Semantics, Logic, Opinions, and Easy Tasks Invited talk

Ivan Habernal
UKP Lab, Technische Universität Darmstadt
habernal@ukp.informatik.tu-darmstadt.de

Abstract

The classical view on argumentation, such that arguments are logical structures consisting of different distinguishable parts and that parties exchange arguments in a rational way, is prevalent in textbooks but nonexistent in the real world. Instead, argumentation is a multifaceted communication tool built upon humans' capabilities to easily use common sense, emotions, and social context. As humans, we are pretty good at it. Computational Argumentation tries to tackle these phenomena but has a long and not so easy way to go. In this talk, I would like to shed a light on several recent attempts to deal with argumentation computationally, such as addressing argument quality, understanding argument reasoning, dealing with fallacies, and how should we never ever argue online.

Proceedings of the Workshop on Computational Semantics beyond Events and Roles (SemBEaR-2018), page 38
New Orleans, Louisiana, June 5, 2018. ©2017 Association for Computational Linguistics

Author Index

Association for Computational Linguistics
209 N. Eighth Street
Stroudsburg, Pennsylvania 18360

ISBN 978-1-5108-6362-0

CURRAN ASSOCIATES INC.
proceedings.com